The Digital Media Reader

Media, Culture, Society and Politics in the Digital Age

Editor: Jonathan Bishop

Foreword: Niki Lambropoulos

Published by The Crocels Press Limited

ISBN: 978-1-78518-006-4

Editor

Jonathan Bishop

Foreword

Niki Lambropoulos

Editorial Board

Jason Barratt

Jeremy McDonagh

Correspondence Address

The Crocels Press Limited, PO Box 674, Swansea, SA1 9NN, Wales, GB

Publication Date

First Published in 2017.

ISBN

978-1-78518-006-4

Disclaimer

All statements contained within the chapters in this book have been checked to ensure they are not defamatory. In the event of any legal action, the editor, editorial board and publisher claim academic privilege with regards to any allegation of defamation.

Contents

Section 3: Society and Politics

The Digital Media Reader

Media, Culture, Society and Politics in the Digital Age

Foreword to the Digital Media Reader

Niki Lambropoulos

Abstract: The editor, Jonathan Bishop, has captured such digital media vast potential and identified 3 major trajectories existing at this era which are evolving and converging into new ways for societies to operate. Such global expansion begins with the media practice from billions of people exposing themselves online. Such digital imitation or authorship transform the personality traits by naturally adapting diverse and new identities, sometimes identical. Such imitation of the digital persona creates trending cultures that shape the societyand naturally, lead to new global habits and politics.

Keywords: Media practice, culture, society, imitation, identity.

Introduction

As this world is increasingly decreasing in size and reach and our abilities and senses are expanded by technological means, people all over the globe compare, choose, shout or observe, imitate or generate ideas, dominate or be free, create or diminish the surrounding world. The Internet, social networks and communities offer the medium that eventually transforms the mediator. We have become digital media seekers, readers, protestors or creators. Digital media platforms mediate to simultaneously unite and divide; reveal, transform and cover intentions and trends; copy, paste, recycle and strengthen what exists; or synthesize and create new possibilities. Hence, the mass data produced by the majority hide the small data trends which, to the competent eye, may eventually transform the 21st Century future. Hence, in a world of infinite possibilities and perspectives, parallel digital universes and identities, digital media define the ways culture and society function by recreating and expanding a minor movement to a typhoon that can change the ultimate ways humans live their lives; politics.

Imitation and creation, thesis antithesis and synthesis of infinite views become the Holy Grail of a brand new world conveying the potential for infinite global movements converging towards any possible trajectory.

In the initial Media Practice section, Shefali Virkar refers to the Impact of the Internet on the Transnational Civil Society Networks. The author discusses the NGOs role, influence and power over the current society via the online platforms. Actions by activists, hacktivists, and cyberprotestors not only do they promote their ideas and activities but also interfere and, in many occasions, alter international relations and political advocacy. The Anonymous Movement is an example of such organisations' contemporary geopolitical power anchored in the online authority for mass reaction via transnational protest and advocacy since the mid-1990s.

The next author, Jonathan Bishop, refers to the informal learning potential for hammering down specific questions answered by communities of experts. Computer mediated communication aids communities of practice members' exchange of information, support, advice and best practices. Such informal education diverse aspects are discussed under the lens of the future educational markets and their effectiveness. In particular, there are references to the cost of chaotic or even onsite advice and consultancy compared to free acquired abilities over the Net.

In their study in Nigeria, Joseph Wilson and Fancis Iloani Arinze refer to citizen journalism so to identify Nigerian trends, concerns and the potential to believe or even add shadows in online information. Nowadays, anyone can be an online journalist on the spot, regardless the truth, ethos or ethics of the information and the journalist. Citizen Journalism and reporting changing lives events directly from the field are connected to citizens' most active participation in the community they actually live and work. Consequently, it is up to the digital writers and readers to deal with the issues of truthfulness, accuracy, objectivity, impartiality, fairness, authentication of sources and public accountability in Nigeria as well as the reasons which they lead to such behaviours.

After Media Practice, the next section is based on the previously discussed pillars and evolves to the Identity and Culture one. Lars Konzack refers to the Internet group Anonymous and generalisation of the Guy Fawkes mask as the direct visual communication symbol conveying the group's message. Since the 17th century Catholic renegade, the mask has become an Internet meme and, additionally, a mask for physical demonstrations in public space. The author presents the ways the Guy Fawkes Mask changed its meaning through the years, and the ways it functions as a meaningful signifier in the digital age.

The next author, Kristen Colbeck, adapts a psychoanalytical approach to analyse the male dominance over female subjects through Internet Creepshots. The paper explores creepshots as non-consensual photographs taken of women in public spaces and shared online via forums directly expressing sexual gratification purposes. The author sheds light on the issue so to increase understanding of the creepshots significance referring to visual pleasure, categorising it as a fetishistic perversion. She argues that such fetishism works in conjunction with voyeuristic scopophilia targeting the male audience. Following this path, the author suggests that creepshots offer power for male domination and consumption.

Lars Konzack., on his quest on the Hero and the Trolls, refers to the case of Mitchell Henderson and the MySpace page commemorating Hendersons suicide. Henderson is the Hero against trolling, also becoming a meme in the troll community known as Anonymous. The author also examines the fact that, depending on the perspective, villains, heroes, tricksters or vigilantes maybe diverse aspects of similar identities adapted by Henderson's followers. Following this perspective, the author conducts a cultural oriented investigation on the Anonymous movement.

Identity and Culture propositions suggest that specific identities are imitated and adapted by vast communities which in turn, shape Society and Politics. Joseph Wilson and Nuhu Gapsiso discuss the social media effect related to the freedom of expression in Nigeria and the ways such collective mind represents national trends. As Nigerians' free expression rights have been manipulated, social media aid Nigerians to articulate and signify their views on all issues, including the country's leaders. The leaders and media organisations utilise the same online means to reach the citizens such a Facebook, to post and comment upon issues of national interest directing people's opinions and beliefs.

Lastly, Ashu M.G. Solo and Jonathan Bishop discuss about conceptualising network politics following the Arab Spring in Africa. Network politics refer to any networking means such the Internet, private networks, cellular networks, telephone networks, radio networks, television networks, to name a few. Networks are utilised as a medium for political communication and engagement; moreover, the governments invoke the networks regulation as such or even manipulate issues derived from such multi-participation and involvement. From this perspective, online network politics become e-politics directed to specific political activities from organizing protests and online petitions to driving revolutions to name a few. The authors also mention digital media applications in politics, as for example robocalling, text messaging, and TV broadcasting, etc. due to their potential for mass influence, impact and citizens' engagement.

Preface to the Digital Media Reader

Jonathan Bishop

Abstract: The Digital Media Reader combines a number of chapters relating to media practice, identity and culture, and society and politics. Its advantage over other textbooks is its focus on contemporary digital media and cultures. A significant number of the chapters relate to the hacktivist movement Anonymous and contemporary events like the Arab Spring and Citizen Journalism.

Keywords: Media practice, identity and culture, and society and politics.

Anonymous

The first chapter in this book by Shefali Virkar looks at the Anonymous Movement in terms of societal networks. In this chapter, Virkar asks whether the Internet is able to augment the effects of those who use it as activists, hacktivists, and cyberprotestors, such as whether it can alter the landscape of international relations and political advocacy. Virkar argues that the Anonymous Movement has successfully harnessed and been impacted by the Internet. In the first chapter of section 2, Lars Konzack explores Anonymous further in terms of the Guy Fawkes mask, which he sees as symbolic of the movement. Konzack explored how the Guy Fawkes Mask changed meaning during history and how it now works as a signifier in the digital age. In the third chapter of section 2, Konzack investigates the case of suicide victim Mitchell Henderson in the context of heroes and villains. Konzack discusses what it means to be a hero and if those that form part of the Anonymous Movement are villains, heroes, tricksters or vigilantes.

Freedom of Expression and Counter-culture

In the second chapter of section 1, I look at the role of informal learning in online communities, with specific reference to Yahoo!Answers and how platforms like it can help ensure the future of markets for dance education. I argue that dance research has to date been focussed on the technical aspects of the discipline and so the physical, cognitive, artistic and social expression aspects of it need to be considered also. By looking into Yahoo!Answers I show how prejudices around sexuality and cultural factors that exist on these platforms can disappear if professional dance educators were to use such platforms as an opportunity to promote the merits of dance education. In the second chapter of section 2, Kristen Colbeck investigates the non-consensual photographic phenomenon of creepshots from a psychoanalytical perspective. Creepshots are taken of women in public places and then shared online for the sexual satisfaction of others. Colbeck describes these as a visual form of fetishistic perversion (fetishistic scopophilia) as well as form of voyeuristic scopophilia. Colbeck argues that those who produce and consume creepshots do so in a subconscious and anonymous fashion in order to remove power from women so as to reduce them to the status of passive sexual objects, even if they are justified by them through the doctrine of free speech. In the first chapter of section 3, Joseph Wilson and Nuhu Gapsiso explore Facebook postings about the popular Nigerian aviation ministry armoured car scandal in order to understand how free speech has changed in Nigeria as a result of social media. The analysis looks at the tone of the posts as well as their overriding position. Joseph Wilson and Nuhu Gapsiso conclude that media organizations use Facebook to generate comments on some issues of national interest and so the platform has enabled greater freedom of speech in Nigeria.

Journalism and Politics

In third chapter of section 1, Joseph Wilson and Fancis Iloani Arinze look at the way journalism has changed so that individuals without specific journalism training are now exercising the functions of journalists, leading to the conceptualization "Citizen Journalism.". Wilson and Arinze argue that this had led to the active participation of members of the society processing information, but not without concerns. They argue that with journalism becoming an "all-comers affair," then problems like fake news are inevitable, as the existence of deficiencies in strictly upholding the tenets of Journalism profession such as truthfulness, accuracy, objectivity, impartiality, fairness, authentication of sources and public accountability are present. The chapter looks at this from the point of view of Nigeria, where citizen journalism raises issues such as ethos or ethics. Finally, in the second chapter of section 3, Ashu M. G. Solo and I look at how politics has changed following the Arab Spring. We propose a concept of network politics as a way of understanding politics in the digital age. Network politics, or 'Polnetics,' refers to politics and networks. Whether these are the Internet, private networks, cellular networks, telephone networks, radio networks, television networks, or anything similar, network politics includes the applications of networks to enable one or more individuals or organizations to engage in political communication. The definition of this field, we argue, should significantly increase the pace of research and development in this important field.

Conclusion

The chapters in the book explore a range of issues that have come about in the age of digital media. Freedom of expression has been challenged by nation states in the past and whilst free speech has been seen by some as a good thing, some of the chapters in this book has shown that there can be adverse consequences as what might be free speech to one person could be considered harmful to another. The use of digital media opens up opportunities for the development of individual potential, with websites like Yahoo!Answers answering common questions that those with uncertainties might ask through to Citizen Journalism, where those with clearly defined opinions can express them without restrictions present in traditional mass media.

Section 1: Media Practice

Society Networks: The Anonymous Movement Unmasked

Shefali Virkar

Abstract: The rise in the number of non-state actors, particularly the emergence of civil society bodies such as NGOs, and the increase of their political influence has thrown up significant questions about how best the Internet and its associated technologies may be harnessed to aid the activities of such organisations. Can the Internet truly augment the effects of those activists, hacktivists, and cyberprotestors seeking to alter the landscape of international relations and political advocacy? This article attempts to answer this question through an examination of the possibly the most iconic, cutting-edge transnational civil society network of the 21st Century: The Anonymous Movement, and the manner in which the collective's participants and constituent elements have successfully harnessed and have in turn been impacted by the Internet and its associated digital platforms and technologies. The research dealt with herein aims to showcase the various intersecting circumstances that help advance Anonymous' contemporary geopolitical power, and in doing so, to contribute to that body of empirical political science which recognises the impact and significance of Information and Communication Technologies and their associated digital platforms on transnational protest and advocacy ever since their development and rapid global proliferation in the mid-1990s.

Keywords: Anonymous, the Internet, Hacktivism, Global Civil Society, Transnational Social Networks.

Introduction

The last quarter of the twentieth century was a time of significant upheaval. Unprecedented advances in computer technology began to collapse vast geographical distances and differences in time, and made it possible for people from different parts of the world to form connections in manner not thought possible before. Centred around information, this technological revolution has today transformed the way in which people around the world think, work, share, and communicate. New technology is changing the world. Although the idea of a communications network spanning the globe is not new, the past three decades have seen the emergence of a vast global network of computers whose effect on the global political arena has been more significant than any previous technological revolution. Following closely on the heels of the advent of the Internet and the rapid global proliferation of the new digital Information and Communication Technologies (ICTs), are important questions concerning the manner in which transnational civil society networks and movements have been able to harness the potential benefits of complex computer systems and of online networking to mount international campaigns for social change. Is the power of the Internet merely a chimera, unable to deliver on its promises?

In attempting to evaluate the significance of the new digital communications technologies, and their role in transforming global social, political, and economic history, this journal research article will take a brief look at possibly the most iconic transnational civil society network of the 21st Century: *The Anonymous Movement*, and the way in which the collective's participants and constituent elements have successfully harnessed and have been impacted by the Internet and its associated digital platforms, "the biggest technological juggernaut that ever rolled" (Gilder, 1999).

This research showcases the various intersecting elements that contribute to Anonymous' contemporary geopolitical power: the ability of the movement to land mainstream media attention, its bold and recognizable aesthetics, its participatory openness, its use of the Internet and the new digital information and communication technologies to self-organise, and the propaganda and misinformation that surrounds the collective's key participants and constituent structural elements. One feature of this cutting-edge political movement stands out: Anonymous' amorphous unpredictability.

Plugging-In: A Brief Background to the Internet

In 1962, an academic at the Massachusetts Institute of Technology (MIT), J.C.R. Licklider, circulated a series of memos elaborating an idea that he called the "Galactic Network", a concept that envisioned "a globally interconnected set of computers through which everyone could quickly access data and programs from any site." He later became the first person to head the computer research programme at the Advanced Research Project Agency (ARPA), a division of the U.S. Department of Defence, where he quickly convinced his successors about of the importance of his idea. His ideas soon converged with those of Paul Baran, an engineer at the American think-tank RAND Corp., whose work stemmed from the concern that a leader of an unfriendly state would be tempted to take advantage of the ease with which military communications could be disrupted, and launch a pre-emptive nuclear strike on the USA circumventing its current digital arrangement. As an alternative to conventional circuit switching technology, therefore, which focused on a single line of communication, Baran suggested the creation of a nationwide network of computers to head off such a catastrophe (Abbate, 2001).

Licklider and Baran's ideas were soon put to the test with the creation of the ARPANET, which commenced operations in the early 1970s. The aim of ARPANET was to make research on military defence related issues efficient by enabling researchers and their government sponsors to share resources without having to physically deliver them. The informal collegial, non-hierarchical working relationships that evolved were the chief cause of ARPANET's early success, ultimately resulting in that of the Internet and its associated technologies as we know it today (Warkentin, 2001). ARPANET's users were also involved in its development: the most significant addition being the introduction of *electronic mail* or *e-mail*, an application that very soon became the most popular feature of the project. From a means of sharing data, the ARPANET thus became a medium of instantaneous and rapid communication.

The late 1980s saw a boom in the sale of personal computers (PCs) and a gradual opening of the Internet to public access. The creation of the World Wide Web in the mid-1990s, following the almost complete privatisation of the ARPANET a few years earlier, completed the transformation of the Internet from a purely defence-related research tool into a popular communication medium that allowed for "information gathering, social interaction, entertainment, and self-expression" as well as the overall interaction of many with many on a global scale. Today, the Internet is shaping and is constantly being shaped by the activities of its users like never before. It is inexpensive and increasingly popular - current estimates suggest that over 2.5 billion people were online as of September 2012, up from a little over 600 million in September 2002 (Internet World Stats, 2012). From its inception, the people and groups who use the Internet have had their own 'agendas, resources, and visions' for its future, making its history 'a tale of collaboration and conflict amongst a remarkable variety of players' (Abbate, 2001).

The explosion in the number of civil society networks dependent on the Internet and its associated technologies over the last few years has been touted as one of the most dramatic and intriguing changes in current world politics (Warkentin, 2001). These groups and their ideas proliferate across borders, and infiltrate nearly all major political arenas, thereby altering the landscape of international political economy with their promise of forging a global civil society that is altogether more just and equitable. Delivering this promise, however, depends on the ability of these groups and networks to communicate with each other quickly over vast expanses of space and time; and it is in this endeavour that new communication technologies, particularly the Internet, have played and will continue to play, a crucial role (Frangonikolopoulos, 2012).

One of the more innovative means used by global civil society for mobilisation and communication has been the Internet, which, since its initial inception and subsequent commercialisation, has provided unprecedented opportunities for the exchange of information outside the control of the dominant mainstream media (Fenton, 2007). The prevalence of such information and resources not other available in the mainstream media, and stemming from alternative sources that may otherwise not be heard or easily accessed, has thus the potential to greatly enhance the quality of action in global civil society and the tools available to actors involved in social and political grassroots struggles.

Political observers and social critics are divided, however, as to the nature and ultimate significance of such citizen networks; with the more optimistic (encompassing a broad spectrum ranging from Gramscians to liberals) seeing these networks as being by-and-large positive expressions of democracy in arenas dominated by nation-states and cross-border companies and as having an ever increasing significance on world affairs (Diebert, 2000). A second line of argument takes a more cautious approach, and vocalises an oft-muted concern that, instead of citizen-focused mass democracy, the global arena will be dotted with millions and millions of niche interests.

More particularly, there are those who associate the advent of the Internet with the idea of the information 'haves' and 'have-nots', and are wary of the consequences ensuing from the so-called 'digital divide' (Zinnbauer, 2001). Finally, there those who believe that, far from being constructive, the Internet is harmful to true global civil society, and in that an increasingly digital society results in a gradual decline in an individual's social circle and in the ultimate destruction of social capital which can only be built up and maintained through continuous face-to-face interaction (Huysman & Wulf, 2004).

This research article examines the significance, structure, and impact that the use of the Internet, Internet-based platforms and technologies, and their opportunities for global networking have had on a radically different type of modern day social activist network: the Anonymous Movement collective, borne out of a sustained and successful series of attempts by informally-organised actors and online group to patrol the World Wide Web in a configuration of behaviours that has since the mid-1990s come to be known as 'trolling' (Virkar, 2014).

Networks and Networking: Connecting For Success

The Internet is altering the landscape of political discourse and advocacy in a way no other technology has done before (Virkar, 2014). It has proved of great use to those who wish to influence foreign policy and the international decision-making process, particularly non-state actors - both individuals and organisations. Cyber activism (otherwise known as Internet activism or *hackitivism*) involves *a normal, non-disruptive use of the Internet in support of an agenda or cause* (Hampson, 2012); such as the use of the Web as an information resource, the construction of user-friendly websites and the posting of material for public viewing, the use of e-mail to disseminate information and electronic publications and letters, and the use of the

World Wide Web as a place to discuss issues, form alliances, and to plan and co-ordinate activities (Jordan & Taylor, 2004).

Coupled with a steadily growing online community, the Internet has become a powerful, inexpensive medium through which ideas and agendas may be communicated (Virkar, 2011). The beauty of the Internet lies in its ability to cross national boundaries, enabling people and organisations from diverse geographical regions to come together to influence foreign policy anywhere in the world (Denning, 2001). Today, many virtual communities are focused on shared political beliefs, and there are a number of websites encouraging online activism (Wall, 2007). The owners of some websites, such as Netaction.com, have even published online 'how-to' guides and training programmes, which *inter-alia* aim to adapt and popularise the use of e-mail, cyberspace networking, internet relay chats, instant messaging and intranets as a means of expanding and sustaining the cyber activist community. As The Virtual Activist training manual proclaims:

> *"… Although you'll need some special skills to build and maintain a Web site, e-mail is easily mastered even if you have little or no technical expertise. If you can read and write and your computer has a modem, you can be a Virtual Activist!"* *(Krause et. al., 2007)*

The successful use of the Internet by civil society organisations lies chiefly in the key organisational process of *networking* (Hampson, 2012). A critical concept, particularly in the context of collective action in the Information Age, the idea of a network is fundamental to an understanding of the dynamics of both online communication and collaboration and to the work that civil society organisations carry on offline (Wall, 2007). In theory, a network consists chiefly of a number of nodes connected to each other in a loose, horizontal, flexible structure that may expand and integrate new nodes and satellites, as long as communication and information flows between the key nodes is maintained (Castells, 1996).

It is easy to infer, therefore, that the emergence of the Internet would greatly benefit the setting up and maintenance of civil society networks in the today's world. Effective use of the Internet and its associated technologies does indeed seem to mitigate traditional difficulties of conventional civil society networks, particularly those issues pertaining to the co-ordination of functions, focusing its resources on specific goals and restraints placed on it due to its size and complexity (Van Laer & Van Aelst, 2010). Scholars of digital society such as Castells often credit the Internet as being the technological basis of form that civil society networks take in the Information Age. Accordingly, the use of technology results in networks having a potent combination of "flexibility and task performance, co-ordinated decision-making and decentralised execution, of individual expression and global horizontal communication which provide a superior form for human action" (Castells, 2001:2).

Networking Dissent: Cyber Activists' use of the Internet

The Internet may be put to a variety of uses by civil society organisations (Arquilla & Ronfeldt, 2001). The five main modes of Internet usage listed and elucidated upon below. These modes are by no means unrelated, and are frequently used in combination by civil society networks to enhance their efficacy (Harwood & Lay, 2001).

Collection

The Internet is a vast storehouse of information, most of it available for free. Today, fact-sheets, policy statements, legislative documents, academic papers, critiques and analyses, and other items relating to a wide variety issues are available for download online. Activists can get hold of whatever material they need at the click of a button, using one of the many search engines, e-mail lists, or chat services available online. News channels providing almost minute-to-minute updates are also available, and prove especially invaluable to groups wishing to monitor ongoing events. In addition, websites provide activists with information on how to use the Internet, its associated applications and digital technologies more effectively.

Publication

Organisations use the Internet to post and distribute information for public consumption. They can create interactive websites that provide global audiences may include fact-sheets, reports, lectures, and interviews. They may publish online journals, create mailing lists, online discussion groups, and bulletin boards. By using the Internet to publish and disseminate information, civil society groups can take advantage of its relatively low costs whilst at the same time reaching out a global audience. The interwoven nature of the World Wide Web, with its links, attachments, and hypertext, enhances its effectiveness as a medium of effective and far-reaching information dissemination.

Dialogue and Debate

E-mail, newsgroups, web forums, chat rooms, and the like provide to civil society multiple forums for the discussion and debate of various issues. For instance, the use of chat rooms has been a subject of robust debate amongst social scientists; with some scholars touting on the one hand virtual discussions as being as good for the building of social capital amongst network members as face-to-face conversations, and with others believing that the only outcome of such impersonal communications is a gradual decline in the quality of interpersonal relationships.

Organising and Mobilising

Advocacy groups use the Internet to increase awareness and mobilise people to rally around an issue. The Net also enables groups to co-ordinate action among members and with other organisations and individuals, across borders and across time-zones. Plans of action may be circulated via e-mail or posted on websites, which exist solely to facilitate better co-ordination between different members of a network.

Lobbying Decision-Makers

The Internet facilitates the lobbying of those in power, and has contributed to the success of many online campaigns. In particular, the use of e-mail has become very popular with, for example, e-mails containing sample protest letters being sent to people on electronic mailing lists, or through the setting up of e-mail boxes by activist groups to gather signatures for petitions. These days, almost everyone who's anyone in the echelons of power and civil society has an e-mail address, and some websites meticulously compile a list of such government officials and urge people to write in to them. It is not clear, however, just how successful such lobbying campaigns are. It is possible that, with e-mail software to block certain types of incoming electronic mail, and the use of standard, automatically generated replies used to respond to electronic petitions, campaign success depends on how well augmented the use of the Internet and associated platforms is with more traditional offline methods; backing the argument made by some that the Internet alone is not an adequate tool for public political movement.

There are, however, several disadvantages or potential drawbacks to the use of the Internet that can limit its usefulness to grassroots groups engaged in political action. More specifically, many of these "downsides" depend on what facets of the Internet are used and the context within which they are applied. Much like the advantages of the Internet discussed above, some have to do with the medium's unique characteristics.

The Internet is a Single Source of Communication

Although the Internet was designed for robustness during the time of emergency, disruptions in the global network of networks can and have occurred. In July 1997, for example, Internet traffic "ground to a halt" across much of the United States because of a freak combination of technical and human errors, forewarning what some Internet experts believed could someday be a more catastrophic meltdown (Chandrasekaran & Corcoran, 1997). Similarly, at a micro-level, Internet crashes and outages are a regular feature of everyday life the world over. Other, older, technologies such as the facsimile and the telephone continue to have an advantage over the Internet in particular situations, particularly if a sender needs immediate acknowledgement or if information is required urgently or covertly or both (Larmer, 1995).

Communications over the Internet Can Be Easily Monitored

Public platforms and Internet websites are easy to monitor and control, particularly by state organisations or individuals with the appropriate technical know-how. Further, private one-to-one electronic messages may be slightly more secure, however, these again can be hacked by anyone with sufficient technical knowledge. Whilst data encryption packages may provide a solution to individuals and organisations exchanging private or classified information, these programmes and their related technologies might for a while remain out of reach of the majority of Internet users (Danitz & Stobel, 2001).

Opponents May Try to Use the Internet for Sabotage

This disadvantage is related to many of the concerns discussed above, but represents a more active use of the Internet by activists, hacktivists and cyber criminals alike to trick, disrupt, or otherwise sow dissension (de Armond, 2001). This is because the Internet allows for anonymity, and makes it possible for provocateurs posing as someone or something else to try to cause dissension or sidetrack the campaign by posting messages for that purpose (Kalathil & Boas, 2010).

Information on the Internet is Unmediated

One of the advantages of the Internet for activists and many other users, of course, is the fact that it allows them to dispense with the traditional filters for news and information (Virkar, 2014). It allows users to self-select information they are interested in and retrieve data in far more detail than available in a newspaper or, certainly, a television programme. This same lack of structure, however, can present dangers, allowing for wide and rapid dissemination of information that is of questionable accuracy, being factually incorrect or propagandistic, including material that is racist, sexist, or otherwise hateful and incendiary (Arquilla & Ronfeldt, 2001).

Access to the Internet and Technical Know-How is Not Equal

Not all who wish to play a role in a campaign for change, have access to the most modern tools of communication, including computers, modems, and the necessary telephone lines or other means to connect to the Internet. As already noted, access to encryption methods that allow for more secure communication may be limited, and technical knowledge concentrated in a small pool of hacktivists bent on causing destruction (Norris, 2001).

The Internet Cannot Replace Face-to-Face Contact

Put simply, the Internet and other communications media cannot replace human interaction. Rather, the Internet has its own set of advantages and disadvantages, with Internet campaigns, because of their decentralized electronic nature, being decidedly unstable (Juris, 2005). Whilst the use of the Internet may supplement face-to-face interactions, it cannot wholly substitute for them as personal interactions constitute nearly-all initial campaigning groundwork (Kalathil & Boas, 2010).

Have transnational civil society networks been able to harness the potential benefits of the Internet and online networking to mount international campaigns for social change? Or is the power of the complex computer systems networking illusory, unable to deliver on its promises? This research article examines the significance, structure, and impact that the use of the Internet, Internet-based platforms and technologies, and its opportunities for global networking have had on a radically different type of modern day social activist network: the Anonymous Movement collective, borne out of a sustained and successful series of attempts by informally-organised actors and online group to patrol the World Wide Web in a configuration of behaviours that has since the mid-1990s come to be known as 'trolling' (Virkar, 2014).

The research paper is divided into three sections. The work commences with a brief overview of the concept of digital networking, moving on to discuss the advantages of the Internet, Internet-based platforms, and digital communications technologies accruing to transnational social networks; in their formation, maintenance, and evolution. The second section, within the framework elucidated, examines in detail The Anonymous Movement and the collective's antecedents. The research first proposes a fairly straightforward, narrative account of Anonymous from 2005 to the present, with key emphasis given to the major events and turning points that define both its constitution and the group's subsequent evolution as a global social movement.

This chronology might be considered particularly necessary given the intrinsic nature of Anonymous as a chimera within the given panopoly of identifiable protest movements online and the high degree of misinformation surrounding it, in direct contrast to the nature of the technological network the collective claims to harness near-exclusively and the civil liberties it professes to defend. The core features of the Anonymous movement, which in turn shed light on its political significance, together with the strengths and weaknesses of Anonymous as a protest movement of recognisable success are also briefly considered. Finally, the research article concludes with an assessment of the broader implications that the Internet revolution holds for civil society networks in the 21st century.

The Anonymous Movement Case Study: Net Resistance = Net Benefits?

The following in-depth case study examines the use of the Internet and its associated platforms and technologies by the global civil society network collective, Anonymous, worldwide. Though seemingly different to the traditional socio-anthropological ideal of transnational civil society groups, the Anonymous Movement nonetheless possesses uncanny similarities to other grassroots protest movements of the digitally networked modern era. Firstly, the Anonymous collective's actions and activist interventions centre around and focus on the impact that the advent of the Internet and the rapid proliferation of Information and Communication Technologies (ICTs) have had on global market forces and globalisation, issues at the heart of recent events in international political economy, and concerns that are bound to increase in importance during the years to come.

Political commentators might also see the rise of the Anonymous movement as proof that transnational citizen networks offer a counter-hegemonic, activist alternative in the grassroots rebellion that has sparked against capitalism, authority, and the State. Secondly, the nature and scale of Anonymous operations has pre-empted, in many instances, resounding if temporary success; Multinational Corporations and national governments have been pushed onto the back foot as a consequence of hacker strike attacks and through the organisation of mass protest, whilst the importance of transnational multilateral agreements and their ensuing discussions lessened as a direct result of operational fallout.

The final common denominator, and the real reason behind the choice of the Anonymous Movement as a case study, is the base fact that the documented, major successes borne out of the committed participation of the collective's constituent elements have been attributed wholly to the Internet and to the rapid transnational proliferation of digital technologies. The high correlation between these successes and the manner of use of the World Wide Web by members of Anonymous, together with the potential lessons that future campaigns might learn from the further elucidation of these experiences are hence the two chief reasons that make the chosen research case study key to a holistic understanding of the role that Internet and its associated technologies play in the shaping of global political architecture.

Anonymous in context: the power and the politics behind the mask

The Anonymous Movement is difficult to pin down and to describe. When considered either as an umbrella term or a rallying cry, the word Anonymous signifies a banner used by individuals and groups to organize diverse forms of Internet-based collective action; ranging from street protests to distributed denial of service (DDoS) campaigns to covert hacking attacks.

Unlike self-professed or registered members of Anonymous, many individual hackers and Internet-based hacktivists work part-time, informally, and surreptitiously. Similarly, organizations whose websites, online databases, and digital repositories have been either hacked or partially compromised usually get to decide whether or not to disclose the precise details of their circumstances and situations to the general public. The Anonymous Movement, in direct contrast, is an informal collective of undisclosed individuals and groups that seeks publicity and attention from the mainstream media before and after every successful action. The fundamental paradox at work here is that state-supported or state-sponsored activism and hacking is altogether much better organized and sufficiently funded and, in most respects, far more powerful than the symbolic action undertaken by the Anonymous collective.

More precisely, a significant proportion of Anonymous participants, known colloquially as "Anons", work independently, whilst yet others work in small teams full-time, or join in as part of a swarm of demonstrators during a flash-mob or other large-scale campaign. Further, the Anonymous Movement lacks the human and financial resources required for the general collective to engage in either the long-term strategic thinking or the planning required to code, to operate, and to sustain military grade hardware and software. More particularly, Anonymous possesses neither the steady income nor the fiscal sponsorship necessary to support a dedicated team tasked with recruiting individuals, coordinating activities, and developing sophisticated computer networks.

Considered within broad framework of its *modus operandi*, Anonymous tends to ride and to amplify the wave of any existing events or activist causes currently trending. However, even if its involvement magnifies and extends the scope of an event or of an occurrence, sometimes so remarkably as to alter the very nature or base significance of the happenstance, tradition dictates that the constituent elements of the Anonymous Movement do not sustain their participation until the bitter end, and that the campaign is eventually discontinued before popular interest wanes.

Oftentimes Anonymous members opt to miss out on the wave completely, or choose to act against the grain of the *vox populi*, particularly when the mainstream media fails to rise entirely to the proffered bait and report especially on the specifics of the movement's operations. Wherein, therefore, lies the real power of Anonymous? Without the wholehearted support of the mainstream media and of the general public, how has the movement in successfully accomplishing its objectives managed to strike such fear into corporations, governments, and other groups and activist collectives?

V For Vendetta and the Rise of Anonymous: 2005 - 2014

Anonymous' ancestry lies in the often obnoxious, occasionally humorous, generally murky, and at times terrifying world of Internet trolling, wherein malicious pranking and cyber-bullying abounds. More precisely, when located within the contextual framework of the movement, the term Internet Trolling is particularly indicative of pathological patterns of digital interaction that consist primarily of acts which deliberately try to chronically distress a person online through the periodic indulgence of frequently inflammatory and abusive behaviour, although usually just to cause disruption without direction and to often do so anonymously (Virkar, 2014).

Internet-based groups and movements like Anonymous have called themselves 'trolls' in order to legitimise their regular abusive behaviour and organised protest action (Bishop, 2014) although in contrast, when more generally surveyed, trolling may be considered as a favourite Internet-based pastime of the bored, the insecure, and the antisocial; usually attempting to bait and to subsequently harm members of the virtual community, collective, or given digital environment into descending to the level of the aggressor or to a similar state of mind.

The Anonymous Movement first made headlines in 2005 when, following the release worldwide of the movie V for Vendetta, the collective adopted the central character's signature mask as the future emblem of the network and as the symbol of a faceless rebel horde (Olson, 2013). First published in 1982, the comic series V for Vendetta charted a masked vigilante's attempt to bring down a fascist British government together with its complicit media (Moore, 2012). Today, it would appear that the central character's charismatic grin has furnished, for members of the Anonymous Movement, a ready-made identity for likeminded, highly motivated protesters (Colter, 2011); one that at once embodies resonances of anarchy, romance, and of theatre – sentiments that are clearly well-suited to the contemporary *cyberactivism* and hacktivist action of the network, from Madrid's Indignados to the Occupy Wall Street movement (Kushner, 2014).

By 2007, Anonymous had become so well known for organised irreverent or casual trolling that Fox News dubbed the collective "the Internet hate machine" (Coleman, 2013). Anonymous mockingly embraced this hyperbolic title (Anonymous, 2007). Six months later, following the adoption of the media epithet by the collective, individuals – primarily participants from 4chan.org – began to operate under the Anonymous banner and to use the imagery, symbolism, and the iconography associated with the movement whilst trolling online and during their appearances at public mass demonstrations and protests (Olson, 2013).

The online trolling campaign against the Church of Scientology was first launched under the banner of Anonymous in 2008, sparked off by a now infamous recruitment video featuring Tom Cruise praising the organisation's efforts to "create new and better realities" (Coleman, 2013). The video, leaked by critics of the church, promptly went viral (Olson, 2013). When the Church of Scientology threatened legal action, members of Anonymous commenced a sustained trolling and DDoS campaign that eventually gave way to Project Chanology (Stone, 2014); a prolonged and earnest political campaign against the church and its supporters hosted on 4chan.org (Fuchs, 2013).

Following a successful start to its hacktivist action, Anonymous in 2009 and 2010 focussed on building on its involvement with Operation Chanology (otherwise known to 4chan.org participants as OpChanology) (Stone, 2014). Trolling activity began to wane by mid-2010, when Anonymous' political portfolio began to diversify following Operation Titstorm, a DDoS attack on the Australian government protesting against legislation aimed at curbing online pornography via the institution of mandatory filters for Internet Service Providers (ISPs) (Coleman, 2013).

In September 2010, self-organising in the name of Internet freedom, a small group of Anons set their eyes on protesting against the Anti-Counterfeiting Trade Agreement (ACTA); the pro-copyright, multilateral agreement on the enforcement of intellectual property rights (Ackerman, 2012). The faction eventually managed to establish a sizable street team of participants and supporters, and a dedicated IRC server in November 2010 called AnonOps (Coleman, 2013).

AnonOps came to the notice of the wider public in December 2010, following the collective's opposition to the recent censorship of the whistle-blowing organisation WikiLeaks (Fuchs, 2013). In response to their refusal to accept payments and donations in the name of the WikiLeaks founder Julian Assange, Anonymous via the AnonOps platform, launched a series DDoS attacks aimed at PayPal, MasterCard, and Visa (Stone, 2014).

By 2011, both Anonymous and WikiLeaks became names emblematic of free speech in the face of censorship (Coleman, 2013). Individual participants began to organise in dedicated AnonOps chat rooms and over channels, teaming up with local activists and hackers in countries like Tunisia, Libya, Egypt, Algeria, and Syria, for a series of campaigns in what came to be known as "Freedom Ops". AnonOps that year also diversified its political portfolio; transitioning to include more subtle Web-based hacking activity against corporate security firm HBGary (Olson, 2013) and database DDoS attacks in opposition to changes made by the San Francisco Bay Area Rapid Transit (BART) (Coleman, 2013).

The winter of 2011-2012 stood witness to yet another increase in online activity amongst members of Anonymous, wherein Anons were in action against a slew of errant corporations and legislative measures (Sembrat, 2011); including the global intelligence firm Stratfor, protests against the looming copyright bill – Stop Online Piracy Act (SOPA), the establishment of a new leaks platform Par:AnoIA (Potentially Alarming Research), a flurry of international operations including OpQuebec and OpIndia, and the Occupy Wall Street movement (Stone, 2014). Most recently, participant hackers of the Anonymous movement have become embroiled in Operation Last Resort which, in 2013, comprised of a series of web defacements and hacks commemorating the memory of activist and hacker Aaron Swartz (Coleman, 2013).

Theorising Anonymous: From Trolling the Lulz to the Theory of Organised Chaos Online

Consider, for example, the birth of the movement as an activist endeavour. Prior to 2008, the name Anonymous was deployed almost exclusively as a generic umbrella term alternative to the locution "trolling", which in Internet parlance refers to the pulling of oft-harmful pranks targeting people and organizations, the desecration and slander of reputations, and the revelation of harmful, humiliating, or personal information online (Virkar, 2014).

During the early years of the Internet, configurations of trolling behaviour were coordinated over online platforms, often on the image board 4chan.org, for the sake of "the lulz"; that is, in order to elicit "malicious laughter" (Virkar, 2014). Anonymous accidentally, if altogether dramatically, however, first cut its teeth and enlarged its repertoire of tactics during the summer of 2008 (Olson, 2013). That year, several of the collective's participants came together over, and the movement sprouted a concerted activist sensibility during, a full-fledged pranking campaign against the Church of Scientology (Bishop, 2014). Two years later, by 2010, distinct and stable activist nodes of the Anonymous Movement had emerged (Coleman, 2013). The name Anonymous was also increasingly being used to herald online activist and hacktivist action and activity, particularly those exploits that often in several ways defied the expectations of both the general public and the mainstream media (Parker, 2014).

At the heart of Anonymous' success as an amorphous, online hacktivist movement or collective, and as staple component of both its contemporary activist programmation and historical development, are continued to be found the key complex network traits of mutability and of dynamism (Coleman, 2013). In consequence, it is altogether difficult to predict, trend, or to forecast *where*, *when*, or *why* the Anonymous movement will strike, *if* a new node will appear in the network, *whether* a campaign will be successful, and *how* the constituent elements of the collective might change direction or alter tactics during the course of an operation (Olson, 2013). A by-product of the Internet, and of the rapid global proliferation of the medium, Anonymous is reputed to rise up and act most forcefully and to garner the most popular support and media coverage whilst defending the fundamental democratic values and human rights associated with this global communications platform, such as free speech and privacy (Fuchs, 2013).

However, the Anonymous movement has repeatedly demonstrated that it is not bound by tradition to either this modus operandi or to any other political imperative (Parker, 2014). Over the last five years, Anonymous has contributed decisively to an astonishing array of *causes celebres*; from the publicization of rape cases in small-town Ohio and Halifax to the aiding and abetting of rebellion in the Arab and the African Spring of 2011 (Kushner, 2014). It is this continuous and constant cycle of growth, circulation, and ongoing metamorphosis that makes the next steps of the Anonymous collective difficult to ascertain and to effectively combat.

Further, despite media reports to the contrary, the Anonymous movement, although nimble, flexible, and emergent, is neither random, shadowy, nor chaotic (Coleman, 2013). Whilst Anonymous, both as a rallying banner under which hacktivists and cyberprotestors gather and as the sum total of the composite individual participants of the collective, may be devilishly unpredictable and difficult to study, the key campaigns of the movement still comprise a number of recognisable core features (Fuchs, 2013).

In contextualizing the Anonymous movement collective within the framework of both recent and historic global socio-political and economic currents and trends, it is altogether unsurprising that a fiery protest movement, closely wedded to the Internet and involving the hypernetworked medium's central features and significant benefits, has arisen at this time in history and in this particular form. As indicated by its very name, Anonymous underlines, highlights, and dramatizes the importance of anonymity and privacy in an era when these civil liberties and other similar fundamental democratic rights are perceived as being rapidly eroded as a consequence of the emergence and development of new, highly sophisticated digital information and communications technology, coupled with a parallel rise in increased government secrecy and in systematic security surveillance.

The Anonymous Movement has also been extremely vocal and forthright on issues of international import during a period of especial, tumultuous global unrest and discontent, evident in the increasing high-frequency of large scale popular uprisings that have occurred across the world; most recently, the 15-M Movement in Spain (2011), the Arab and African Spring (2011), and the Occupy Movement in the U.S.A. (2011) (Kushner, 2014). Over the last two years, in keeping with global economic and historical cyclical convention, sharp inequalities in economic performance the world over have been met by a tide of grassroots protest activity online (Virkar, 2014).

Whilst remaining independent and distinct from this historical tradition, Anonymous considers itself still part and parcel of the general global trend; symbolically showcasing its conception of the ideal for privacy and other civil liberties, together with acting as both the popular face of global digital unrest and the rallying cry across these various protest movements. In this manner, Anonymous demonstrates and exercises the power of symbolic Internet-based digital engagement within the broader political contextual framework of direct social action.

The Logic of Anonymous: Global Civil Society And 'The Weapons Of The Geek'

Relying on a fairly predictable stereotype, most commentators, from scholars to field practitioners and working professionals, usually think of the Anonymous movement as consisting of an evasive and shadowy group of hackers (Parker, 2014). This truncated description often runs contrary to discussions of sociological reality, to the very real social composition of the collective (Fuchs, 2013). Although Anonymous is certainly home to hackers of various hues, a great many Anons are neither proficient at programming nor are difficult to find (Parker, 2014). True to fact, if one wants to talk with Anonymous participants, simply log onto one of their IRC networks (Kushner, 2014).

della Porta and Diani (1999) define social movements as possessing four major characteristics: social movements are (1) informal networks, based upon (2) shared beliefs and a sense of solidarity, wherein (3) constituent actors mobilize around (4) controversial, contentious, and emotive issues, through (5) the frequent employ of various forms of protest (della Porta & Diani 1999). In other words, social movements might be defined as "networks of informal interactions between a plurality of individuals, groups and/ or organizations, engaged in political or cultural conflicts, on the basis of shared collective identities" (Diani 1992: 13).

In studying hypermodern global social movements like Anonymous, Fuchs (2006) further identifies a number of key defining aspects necessary to the advancement of this typography of actor-network relationship. These include the presence of:

societal problems; the negation of dominant values, institutions and structures; dissatisfaction; adversaries; shared collective identities; orientation towards social change; triggers of protest, their repercussions, and the effects of contagion; network mobilization through protest practices and collective action; protest methods and their deployment; and extra-parliamentary politics and politicking.

A specific characteristic of Anonymous is that the collective considers itself to be at once a *global social movement* and an *anti-movement* (Fuchs, 2013); its activist interventions and political action are based upon and constituted out of a shared common identity and group identification with a common set of basic values which include fundamental civil liberties and freedom of the Internet that results in protest practices online and offline against common adversaries, whilst simultaneously involving many of the regular participants on Anonymous platforms there to engage primarily in individual play and in entertainment (Kushner, 2014). In this respect, Anons participate in collective action predominantly 'for the lulz'; traditionally to elicit malicious fun for the participant-users concerned (Virkar, 2014), but from time-to-time to convert individual action into collective political intervention (Bishop, 2014).

In keeping with the collective's reputation as a global social or protest movement, Anonymous' political actions are grounded in a number of shared, pivotal, base political values that are elucidated upon in *5 Principles: An Anonymous Manifesto*, the movement's core political polemic (Fuchs, 2013).The group's stated values might be further summarised as being a struggle for an "open, fair, transparent, accountable and just society", in which information is "unrestricted and uncensored", and wherein Anonymous in central to the upholding of citizens' "rights and liberties" and to underwriting of a guarantee to strengthen the "privacy of citizens" so that "citizens shall not be the target of any undue surveillance" (Coleman, 2013). Anonymous further operates on the basis of three concurrent principles: that (1) the media should not be attacked; that (2) critical infrastructure should not be attacked; and that (3) individual action should work for justice and freedom (Fuchs, 2013).

Scholars of global civil activism and their practitioner-activist counterparts each possess their own separate interpretations and judgements concerning these basic, fundamental values of freedom and justice set down in the Anonymous Manifesto. The overall impression of Anonymous when examined from the perspective of the scholarly community is that of a collective functioning according to exceedingly loose principles and moral standards, very much unlike a highly formalised party-political programme (Fuchs, 2013). While this degree of flexibility might also be characteristic of other contemporary social movements, Anonymous diverges from them in maintaining a high level of anonymity amongst, for, and within its various activists and differing protest practices (Parker, 2014).

Conventional social movements, in the manner of political party networks, tend to encourage and be sustained through the establishment and maintenance of personal relations, face-to-face meetings, discussions, and actions (Fuchs, 2006). Similarly, their campaigns are often focused on the targeting of strategic adversaries (Fuchs, 2013.). In contrast, the highly decentralized and informal character of the Anonymous network often results in multiple independent and parallel campaigns that can become networked and coordinated but can also exist independently (Coleman, 2013), wherein people who share in a basic value are allowed to declare an action in the movement's name (Kushner, 2014).

Anonymous, similar to its other global civil society counterparts, conforms to permutations in "logics of action" that might be combined in different ways (della Porta & Diani 2006; Fuchs, 2013). Within this framework, Anonymous' chosen methods of protest are unconventional, if not hypermodern. Protests can take place either online, primarily as conversation in Internet Relay Chat (IRC) rooms or through the hacking of websites, the publishing personal of data, DDoS attacks, and/ or offline, as street protests or mass demonstrations (Fuchs, 2013). The logic of the Anonymous movement is that of collective action organised and executed at a distance (Sembrat, 2011). The first logic of action requires, therefore, that the collective achieve temporal synchronicity, difficult to co-ordinate when there are distributed actions conducted over the Internet remotely (Fuchs, 2013). The second logic of protest action associated with the movement is that which coordinated and planned online, but which makes use of temporal and spatial co-presence both on- and offline (Kushner, 2014).

Irreverent Activism and the Notion of Digital Direct Action

Invented in 1989, Internet Relay Chat (or *IRC*) is still used by geeks and hackers to develop collaborative software and, as its name suggests, to chat or to converse (Coleman, 2013). IRC, unlike other rich-text media, consists of only bare-bones functionality: the medium is entirely text-based, generally free of brightly colour, icons, cute noises, and interaction is conducted in-window with its own mix of text commands and norms of communication (Glenny, 2011). In being ideal for real-time communication and for coordinating protest action and operations, many Anons become regulars within various stable IRC networks, where they converse and find fellowship on public or private channels (Olson, 2013). In many regards, these channels function similar to online social clubs, open round the clock. Anons aren't required to collaborate over IRC (Stone, 2014); some prefer to act alone, whilst others turn to Web forums, open platforms like Twitter or .delicious, or to other chat protocols (Olson, 2013). Truly illegal activities are orchestrated over by-invite-only, encrypted communication channels (Glenny, 2011).

Hackers, from programmers to security researchers to system administrators, are essential to maintaining the lifeblood of Anonymous' networks: they erect and maintain communications infrastructure, infiltrate servers to expose weak security, or in their hunt for information, leak data (Parker, 2014). Nevertheless, compared to other spheres of hacker activity wherein contributions, and often respect, require and are determined by the prevalent degree of technical skill, Anonymous is more participatory, in that what sustains the movement is its dynamism and flexibility (Kushner, 2014). No particular abilities are advertised as being required. Whilst hackers obviously wield more technical power, and their opinions carry weight online, this subset of participants do not either erect barriers to entry or control the evolution of Anonymous (Coleman, 2013).

Individuals without technical skills may participate collectively through actively recruiting new volunteers, writing press communiqués, giving media interviews on IRC, designing propaganda posters, editing videos, and by mining information that is publicly available but difficult to access (Kushner, 2014). Organizers also emerge from within the ranks to advise, inspire, and to corral troops; and sometimes to broker between different groups and networks in the formation of inter-network *ad hoc* teams (Parker, 2014). Although the structure of the Anonymous network may at times appear to be chaotic, participants rarely choose targets at random

(Olson, 2013). Operations tend to be reactive, whereby existing local, regional, and international events and causes can trigger action from Anonymous groups worldwide (Kushner, 2014). Given this, all types of collective operations can usually be linked to a particular IRC network, including *AnonOps*, *AnonNetor*, *Voxanon* or related Twitter accounts, such as *@OpLastResort*, dedicated to the particular operation at hand (Olson, 2013).

In order to be part of Anonymous, therefore, one needs to simply self-identify as being Anonymous. No single group or individual can dictate the manner and direction in which the name or the iconography of the Anonymous movement is used, much less claim legal ownership over its pseudonyms, aliases, icons, and actions. The Weapons of the Geek remain out of public reach.

We Are Legion: Anonymous, From Flash Crowd To Slashdot

The Anonymous Movement considers itself as being nothing short of "21st century enlightenment" personified (Fuchs, 2013). True. The collective cannot be simply described as being a mere 'part-and-parcel' of the enlightenment dialectic of modern-day, turn-of-the-century informational capitalism (Taylor, 2013). In both demanding and opposing the very rights and values that capitalism, its constitutions, and its adherents profess, the movement and its constituent participatory elements have demonstrated and have publicly disclosed – through positions taken and held with relation to the methods of direct action employed, means of indirect intervention resorted to, and stance taken in terms of moral reasoning – the contradictions inherent within Anonymous' equation with the general *vox populi* and with hypermodern-day society at large; manifest and expressed in terms of degrees of freedom observable and the differences intrinsic to the spectrum of conventional liberal ideology.

Only a handful of actions performed under the banner of the Anonymous movement have been atypical and radically non-conformist (Parker, 2014). Hence, whilst predictions of chaos unleashed by malicious or maladjusted hackers loom large within the ambit of the state's anxieties regarding Anonymous, they remain largely unrealized. That's not to say that all of Anonymous' operations are laudable, effective, or, indeed, publicly acknowledged. On the contrary, as the base character and tactics of each Anonymous operation are usually distinct, blanket moral judgments are hard to make, and related pronouncements tend to be overly simplistic as against either nuanced or sophisticated (Fuchs, 2013).

The majority of individual Anons never break the law; however, since Anonymous cannot and will not generally police participants as a collective, it's possible that some may do so (Stone, 2014). Further, despite the given unpredictability of the movement, its past actions provide no sound basis for predicting the future. Nonetheless, reckless operations meant to endanger lives have, thus far, never been part of Anonymous' overt moral calculus or tactical repertoire (Coleman, 2013). Certain factions have certainly done so covertly; wherein any vulnerability has been exploited, and any advantage generally leveraged (Ackerman, 2012).

Unlike other criminal groups who want to remain hidden, Anonymous seeks the limelight regularly to publicize its campaigns and the direct action employed therein (Olson, 2013). Both the mainstream and grassroots media also contribute towards the achievement of this public relations agenda, frequently featuring and sometimes highlighting the more controversial acts of the collective within their reportage and, in doing so, invariably boosting the Anonymous movement's global profile and public image (Kushner, 2014).

Partly as a consequence of its maverick image, and in part the nature and scale of its transgressive antics, Anonymous has attracted significant international attention, sometimes admiration, sometimes caution, and oftentimes fear (Parker, 2014). As an entity, the Anonymous collective intends itself to be amorphous, indestructible, slippery, evasive, and even invisible; if at the same time both international and, within its sphere of influence, omnipotent (Fuchs, 2013). Anonymous' overarching principle of organisational structure — *anonymity*, or more technically put, *pseudonymity* — makes it difficult to tell just how many people are involved overall (Coleman, 2013).

As a result, misinformation regarding Anonymous abounds. Some of it is self-created, some has been foisted upon the movement. Although core participants exist and chat channels are overtly dedicated to reporters and to movement reportage, Anonymous reputed to comprise a shifting cast of characters (Ackerman, 2012). Some individuals routinely change their online nicknames (Olson, 2013). Catching up can prove frustrating, and certainly time consuming once a participant leaves for a spell, even more so for an outside observer (Kushner, 2014). Journalists, even those reporting for reputable news outlets, have at times incorrectly identified and typecast Anonymous direct action (Parker, 2014).

To disguise itself further, deflect media attention, and to even confound anonymous participants internal to and embedded within the collective, Anonymous also seeds false propaganda (Taylor, 2014). It can be hard, at times, to distinguish fib from fact, truth from lies. However, this obfuscation only adds to the collective's mystique and, thence, to the innate power of The Anonymous Movement.

Conclusions: Anonymous and the Future of the Internet

Never before in the history of mankind has any invention shot from obscurity to global fame in quite the way the Internet has. Never before has any new technology given us a peek into the future in quite the same manner: a glimpse into a highly interconnected world where the cost of transmitting and accessing an infinite amount of information is reduced to virtually nothing, where material boundaries are no longer limits to human action, and constrained physical space is replaced by a virtual *'cyberspace'* which is not subject to traditional hierarchies and to conventional power relations. And where there is place for all regardless of gender, sexual orientation, nationality, ethnicity, or religion. In short, the Internet promises us a rapid movement towards a just and prosperous world, and the development of a truly global, comprehensively networked civil society.

At the same time, there are roadblocks to be overcome if the Internet, together with the medium's associated applications and platforms, is to deliver on its promises. Contrary to the claims of cyber romantics, equality and empowerment are not inevitable consequences of the use of technology and its application to day-to-day living. The present bias of the Internet towards the West, with the predominance of English as the major *lingua franca* online, reinforces the existing global digital divide and reflects the lopsided power relationships currently prevalent in contemporary world politics. This imbalance is a formidable barrier to a truly international and hypernetworked civil society, and there is no guarantee that alteration to modern society will see it rectified in the near future. Furthermore, issues of Internet regulation and security have, particularly after its effective use by criminal and terrorist networks such as Al-Qaeda, become hotly debated issues in both scholarly and practitioner circles.

In the Information Age, societies and civilisations find themselves highly interconnected. The days of closed-door negotiations and secret repression are drawing to an end. As many national governments and supranational agencies have found out the hard way, the digital technology has empowered those Non-Governmental Organisations, protest movements, and advocacy groups that have embraced the Internet and which are now electronically networked across borders. Information technology has become, and looks set to remain, a critical ingredient of networking activity and mass protest in today's world. Civil society networks, buttressed by the power of the Internet, information and communications technologies, and digital platforms, have found themselves able to defy existing boundaries. We can no longer remain isolated from the networks of power and resistance that criss-cross and envelop our increasingly interconnected world.

Transnational movements of the 21st century enlightenment have recognised this, and are increasingly expanding their presence on the Internet. From the more traditional movements of the era such as the Labour Movement, to more recent ones such as the Campaign Against Climate Change, and then to hypermodernity of the Anonymous Movement collective, there is a growing acknowledgement of the Internet's dynamism and versatility, and an increased recognition of its advantages and contribution to the shaping of modern society in its role as a medium of international communication. The ease with which information can be exchanged, together with the fluency of the logistics planned between partners thousands of miles apart, promises activists new opportunities for vigorous coalition-building and other similarly related civil rights protest and advocacy activities. By the same logic, the Internet has also become an increasingly important tool for facilitating and for cementing the social relations that serve as the basis for global civil society.

The contemporary world is in the midst of a historical change. The Information Revolution has given way today to new powers and to new responsibilities and to a whole new host of unrecognisable actors who, through embracing the Internet and digital technologies, are fast becoming central to the new, electronically hypernetworked modern-day civil society. Whilst Internet access in the developed world still far outstrips that of the developing world, predictions made of the expected growth in the number of Internet users online worldwide annually remain phenomenal, and the potential and promise of the Internet as a tool to combat underdevelopment and inequality in the future is yet considered immense. The Internet today, in its avatar as the chief Weapon within the Armoury of the Geek, constitutes a significant part of global socio-political and economic interactions, and will continue to play an increasingly important role in the shaping of world politics and current affairs in the years to come.

References

Arquilla, J. & D. Ronfeldt (2001), *Networks and Netwars: The Future of Terror, Crime, and Militancy*. Santa Monica, C.A.: RAND Publications.

Bishop, J. (2014). My Click is My Bond: The Role of Contracts, Social Proof, and Gamification for Sysops to Reduce Pseudo-Activism and Internet Trolling. In J. Bishop (Ed.), *Gamification for Human Factors Integration: Social, Education and Psychological Issues* (pp. 1–16). Hershey, PA: IGI Global.

Blatherwick, D.E.S. (1987). *The International Politics of Telecommunications*, Research Series #68, Institute of International Studies. Berkley, C.A.: University of California.

Cairncross, F. (1997). The Death of Distance: How the Communications Revolution is Changing Our Lives. Boston, M.A.: Harvard Business School Press.

Castells, M. (1996). The Information Age: Economy. Society and Culture Volume 1- The Rise of the Network Society. Oxford: Blackwell Publishing.

Castells, M. (2001). The Internet Galaxy: Reflections on the Internet, Business and Society, Oxford: Oxford University Press.

Chandrasekaran, R. & E. Corcoran (1997). Human Errors Block E-Mail, Web Sites in Internet Failure: Garbled Address Files From Va. Firm Blamed. *The Washington Post,* July 18, 1997. p. A1.

Cleaver Jr., H. M. (1998). The Zapatista Effect: The Internet and the Rise of an Alternative Political Fabric. *Journal of International Affairs, 51*(2), 621-640.

Coleman, G. (2013). Anonymous in Context: The Politics and Power Behind the Mask. *Internet Governance Papers – Paper No. 3, September 2013.* The Centre for International Governance Innovation (CIGI).

Colter, A. (2011). V for Vendetta Inspires Anonymous, Creator David Lloyd Responds. Comics Alliance Online, 04 August 2011.

Conway, S., Combe, I., & D. Crowther (2003). Strategizing Networks of Power and Influence: the Internet and the Struggle over Contested Space. *Managerial Auditing Journal, 18*(3), 254-262.

Danitz, T. & W.P. Stobel (2001). Networking Dissent: Cyber Activists Use The Internet to Promote Democracy in Burma. In J. Arquilla & D. Ronfeldt (eds.) *Networks and Netwars: The Future of Terror, Crime, and Militancy* (pp. 129-170), Santa Monica, C.A.: RAND Publications.

de Armond, P. (2001). Netwar in the Emerald City: WTO Protest Strategy and Tactics. In J. Arquilla & D. Ronfeldt (eds.) *Networks and Netwars: The Future of Terror, Crime, and Militancy* (pp. 201-238), Santa Monica, C.A.: RAND Publications.

Deibert, R. J. (2000). International Plug 'n Play?: Citizen Activism, the Internet and Global Public Policy. *International Studies Perspectives, 1*(3), 255-272.

Deibert, R. J. (2002). The Politics of Internet Design: Securing the Foundations for Global Civil Society Networks, *Paper presented at the Institute of Intergovernmental Relations.*

della Porta, D. & M. Diani (1999). *Social Movements: An Introduction, First Edition.* Malden, M.A.: Blackwell Publishing.

Denning, D. E. (2001). Activism, Hactivism and Cyberterrorism: The Internet as a Tool for Influencing Foreign Policy. In J. Arquilla & D. Ronfeldt (eds.) *Networks and Netwars: The Future of Crime, Terrorism and Militancy* (pp. 171-199), Santa Monica, C.A.: RAND Publications.

Diani, M. (1992). The Concept of Social Movement. *The Sociological Review, 40*(1), 1-25.

Fenton, N. (2007). Contesting Global Capital, New Media, Solidarity and the Role of a Social Imaginary. In B. Cammaerts & N. Carpentier (eds) *Reclaiming the Media* (pp. 225-242), Brussels: ECREA Series - Intellect.

Frangonikolopoulos, C.A. (2012). Global Civil Society and Deliberation in the Digital Age. *International Journal Electronic Governance, 5*(1), 11–23.

Fuchs, C. (2006). The Self-Organization of Social Movements. *Systemic Practice and Action Research, 19*(1), 101-137.

Fuchs, C. (2013). The Anonymous Movement in the Context of Liberalism and Socialism. *Interface: A Journal For and About Social Movements, 5*(2), 345-376.

Glenny, M. (2011) *DarkMarket: CyberThieves, CyberCops, and You*. London: The Bodley Head.

Hampson, N.C.N. (2012). Hacktivism: A New Breed of Protest in a Networked World. *Boston College International & Comparative Law Review, 35*(2), 511-542.

Harris, E (1999). Web Becomes a Cybertool for Political Activists. *Wall Street Journal*, 5th August 1999, p. B11.

Harwood, P. G., & L. J. Celeste (2001). Surfing Alone: The Internet as a Facilitator of Social and Political Capital?. *Paper prepared for delivery at the 2001 Annual Meeting of American Political Science Association*, Aug-Sept. 2001.

Huysman, M. & V. Wulf (2004). *Social Capital and Information Technology*, Cambridge M.A.: M.I.T. Press.

Johnston, J. & G. Laxer (2003). Solidarity in the Age of Globalization: Lessons from the Anti-MAI and Zapatista Struggles. *Theory and Society*, *32*(1), 39-91.

Jordan, T. & P.A. Taylor (2004). *Hacktivism and Cyberwars: Rebels with a Cause?*, London: Routledge Press.

Juris, J.S. (2005). The New Digital Media and Activist Networking within Anti−Corporate Globalization Movements. *The ANNALS of the American Academy of Political and Social Science, 597*(1), 189-208.

Kalathil, S. & T. C. Boas (2010). *Open Networks, Closed Regimes: The Impact of the Internet on Authoritarian Rule*. Washington, D.C.: Carnegie Endowment for International Peace.

Koliba, C. (2000). Collaboration, Technical Assistance and Interactive Media: Trends in U.S. Civil Society. *Institute of Development Studies Civil Society and Governance Case Study Papers (USA) #20*.

Krause, A., Stein, M., Clark, J., Chen, T., Li, J., Dimon, J., Kanouse, J. & J.Herschman (2006). The Virtual Activist 2.0: A Training Guide. *NetAction.Org.*

Kraut, R., Patterson, M. Lundmark, V., Kiesler, S., Mukhopadyay, T., & W. Scherlis (1998). Internet Paradox: A Social Technology That Reduces Social Involvement and Psychological Well-Being?. *American Psychologist, 53*(9), 1017-1031.

Kumar, C. (2000). Transnational Networks and Campaigns for Democracy. In A. M. Florini (ed.) *The Third Force: The Rise of Transnational Civil Society* (pp. 115-142). Tokyo: Japan Centre for International Exchange and Washington D.C.: Carnegie Endowment for International Peace.

Kushner, D. (2014). The Masked Avengers: How Anonymous Incited Online Vigilantism from Tunisia to Ferguson. *The New Yorker*, 08 September 2014.

Longworth, R.C. (1999). Activists on Internet Reshaping Rules for Global Economy. *Chicago Tribune*, 5 July, 1999.

McChesney, R. W., Wood, E. M., & J. B. Foster (1998). Capitalism and the Information Age: The Political Economy of the Global Communications Revolution. New York, N.Y.: Monthly Review Press.

Moore, A. (2012). Viewpoint: V for Vendetta and the Rise of Anonymous. *BBC News Online – Technology*, 10 February 2012.

Norris, P. (2001). Digital Divide: Civic Engagement, Information Poverty, and the Internet, Cambridge: Cambridge University Press.

Olson, P. (2013). WE ARE ANONYMOUS: Inside the Hacker World of LulzSec, Anonymous, and the Global Cyber Insurgency. London: Random House.

Organisation for Economic Co-operation and Development (1997). *Towards A Global Information Society – Global Information Infrastructure, Global Information Society: Policy Requirements*. Paris: Organisation for Economic Cooperation and Development.

Parker, C. (2014). Anonymous Unmasked. *The Huffington Post*, 01 April 2014.

Sembrat, E. (2011) How to Respond and Build Around Hacker Communities. *IS 8300 – Disaster Recovery and Contingency Planning, Fall 2011*, October 21, 2011.

Stone, J. (2014). What Is Anonymous? 'Hacktivist' Involvement In Mike Brown Shooting Proves Vigilante Justice Is Now Routine. *International Business Times* (Online), 15 August 2014.

Surman, M. & K. Reilly (2003). Appropriating the Internet for Social Change: Towards the Strategic Use of Networked Technologies by Transnational Civil Society Organisations. *Social Science Research Council Report, November 2003.*

Taylor, B.C. (2013). *No More Suffering Fools.* Rahleigh, N.C.: PostPaper/Lulu Enterprises Inc.

Tehranian, M. & R. Falk (1999). Global Communication & World Politics: Domination, Development and Discourse. London: Lynne Rienner Publications.

The Economist (2001). Globalisation: Making Sense of An Integrating World. London: Profile Books Ltd.

Uimonen, P. (2003). Networks of Global Interaction. *Cambridge Review of International Affairs*, 16(2), 273-286

Van Laer, J. & P. Van Aelst (2010). Internet and Social Movement Action Repertoires. *Information, Communication, & Society.* 13(8), 1146-1171.

Virkar, S. (2011). The Politics of Implementing e- Government for Development: The Ecology of Games Shaping Property Tax Administration in Bangalore City. Unpublished Doctoral Thesis. Oxford: University of Oxford.

Virkar, S. (2014). Trolls Just Want To Have Fun: Electronic Aggression within the Context of e-Participation and Other Online Political Behaviour in the United Kingdom. *International Journal of E-Politics*, 5(4), 21-51.

Walter, A. (2000). Unravelling the Faustian Bargain: Non-State Actors and the Multilateral Agreement on Investment. *Working Paper 4th Draft*, London School of Economics and Political Science, August 2000.

Wall, M. A. (2007). Social Movements and Email: Expressions of Online Identity in the Globalization Protests. *New Media Society, 9*(2), 258-277.

Wartenkin, C. (2001). Reshaping World Politics: NGOs, the Internet and Global Civil Society. Oxford: Rowman and Littlefield.

Zinnbauer, D. (2001). Internet, Civil Society and Global Governance: The Neglected Political Dimension of the Digital Divide. *Information and Security: An International Journal, 7,* 45-64.

Documentation

Ackerman, E. (2012). Why Anonymous is Winning Its War on Internet Infrastructure. www.forbes.com. Available at: http://www.forbes.com/sites/eliseackerman/2012/02/21/why-anonymous-is-winning-its-war-on-internet-infrastructure/ (Accessed on: 20/01/2015).

Internet Society (2013). All About the Internet: A Brief History of the Internet. Available at: http://www.isoc.org/internet/history/brief.shtml#Origins (Accessed: 2nd October 2013).

Additional Reading

Berger, M. T. (2001). Romancing the Zapatistas: International Intellectuals and the Chiapas Rebellion. *Latin American Perspectives, 28*(2), 149-170

Box, L. & Engelhard, R. (2001). International Civilateral Transformations: ICTs in Development Co-operation. *Paper prepared for the HIVOS Symposium 2001.* Available at: www.hivos.nl/downloads/boxdoc.pdf (Accessed: 7th February 2013).

Braiker, B. (2008). 'Anonymous' Takes on Scientology. *Newsweek,* 02 August 2008. Available at: http://www.newsweek.com/anonymous-takes-scientology-93883 (Accessed on: 10th February 2015).

Centre for Science and Environment (India) (2013). Global Environmental Negotiations Factsheet: Fact 10 - The Multilateral Agreement on Investment. Available at: http://www.cseindia.org/html/eyou/geg/factsheet/fact10.pdf (Accessed: 4th February 2013).

Cleaver Jr., H. M. (1995) 'The Zapatistas and the Electronic Fabric of Study', Available: http://www.eco.utexas.edu/faculty/Cleaver/zaps.html (Accessed: 2nd November 2013).

Cleaver Jr., H. M. (1999). The Zapatistas in Cyberspace: A Guide to Analysis and Resources. Available at: http://www.eco.utexas.edu/faculty/Cleaver/zapsincyber.html (Accessed: 7th May 2013).

della Porta, D. & M. Diani (2006). *Social movements: An Introduction, Second Edition*. Malden, M.A.: Blackwell Publishing.

Drohan, M. (1998). How the Net Killed the MAI: Grassroots Groups Used Their Own Globalization to Derail Deal. *The Globe and the Mail*, 28th April 1998.

Froehling, O. (1997). The Cyberspace War of 'Ink and Internet' in Chiapas, Mexico. *Geographical Review*, *87*(2), 291-307.

Gilbreth, C. & Otero, G. (2001). Democratisation in Mexico: The Zapatista Uprising and Civil Society. *Latin American Perspectives*, *28*(119/4), 7-29.

Joint NGO Statement on the Multilateral Agreement on Investment (MAI) (1997). Delivered to the Organisation for Economic Cooperation and Development, NGO/OECD Consultation, Paris, 27 October, 1997. Available at: http://bocs.hu/igaz-a-1.htm (Accessed: 2nd October 2013).

Kobrin, S. J. (1998). The MAI and the Clash of Globalisations. *Foreign Policy*, *112*(1), 97-109.

Kobrin, S.J. (2012). The Multilateral Agreement on Investment. In G.Ritzer (ed.) *The Wiley-Blackwell Encyclopedia of Globalisation*, London: Blackwell Publishing Ltd.

Kurtz, J. (2002). NGOs, the Internet and International Economic Policy Making: The Failure of the OECD Multilateral Agreement on Investment. *The Melbourne Journal of International Law*, 3(2), 213-246.

Martinez-Torres, M.E. (2001). Civil Society, the Internet, and the Zapatistas. *Peace Review: A Journal of Social Justice*, 13(3), 347-355.

Mora. M. (2008). Zapatista Anti-Capitalist Politics and the "Other Campaign": Learning from the Struggle for Indigenous Rights and Autonomy. In R. Stahler-Sholk, H. E. Vanden & G. D. Kuecker (eds.) *Latin American Social Movements in the Twentieth Century; Resistance, Power, and Democracy* (pp. 151-164), London: Rowman and Littlefield.

Neumayer, E. (1999). Multilateral Agreement on Investment: Lessons for the WTO from the Failed OECD Negotiations. *Wirtschaftspolitische Blätter*, 46(6), 618-628.

O'Brien, R. (2002). Global Civil Society Networks Online: Zapatistas, the MAI and Landmines. *Published in May 2002*. Available at: http://www.web.net/~robrien/papers/civsocnets.html#_Toc535832619 (Accessed: 2nd October 2013).

Olesen, T. (2004). The Transnational Zapatista Solidarity Network: An infrastructure Analysis. *Global Networks*, 4(1), 89-107.

Organisation for Economic Co-operation and Development (2013). The MAI: Documentation from the Negotiations. *OECD, Paris*. Available at: http://www1.oecd.org/daf/mai/ (Accessed: 20th October 2013).

Protest.Net (2013). *Protest.Net*. Available at: www.protest.net, (Accessed: 2th October 2013).

Robberson, T. (1995). Mexican Rebels Using a High Tech Weapon. *Washington Post,* 20th February 2005, p. A1.

Russell, A. (2001). The Zapatistas and Computer-Mediated Peace. *Peace Review: A Journal of Social Justice, 13*(3), 357-363.

Russell, A. (2005). Myth and the Zapatista Movement: Exploring a Network Identity. *New Media Society, 7*(1), 559-577.

Sforza, M., Nova, S. & M. Weisbrot (1996). Writing a Constitution of a Single Global Economy: A Concise Guide to the MAI – Supporters and Opponents' Views. *Preamble Collective.* Available at: http://www.cepr.net/documents/publications/maioverv.html#N_2 (Accessed: 2nd October 2013).

Smith, P. & E. Smythe (1999). Globalization, Citizenship and Technology: The MAI Meets the Internet. *Canadian Foreign Policy, 7*(2), 83-105.

The Economist (1999). *Economics: Making Sense of the Modern Economy.* London: Profile Books.

University of Toronto (2013). The Multilateral Agreement on Investment. *G8 Information Centre.* Available at: http://www.g7.utoronto.ca/ (Accessed: 3rd October 2013).

Virkar, S. (2014). Re-engaging the Public in the Digital Age: e-Consultation Initiatives in the Government 2.0 Landscape. *Encyclopedia of Information Science and Technology, 3rd Edition* (pp. 427-435). Hershey, P.A.: IGI Global Inc.

Ensuring the future of markets for dance education: Considering the role of informal learning through the prism of Yahoo!Answers

Jonathan Bishop

Abstract: Current dance research has been focussed much around technical aspects to dance and the need for public policy makers to consider dance education as a fundamental part of the subjects relating to physical, cognitive, artistic and social expression. For dance education to remain relevant in times of austerity and economic hardship, dance educators need to look behind the classroom in order to create a need for formal dance education. This paper presents a research investigation into Yahoo!Answers – a social network where those who know about subjects share their knowledge with those who want to know. The paper shows how many of the barriers to participation in dance – such as prejudices around sexuality and cultural factors – can be overcome if professional dance educators see such platforms as places of informal learning, where they can encourage those interested in dance to take up dance education.

Introduction

It has been argued that dance education is in desperate need for reform, both at a cultural and a technical level (Risner 2010, 95-110). In times of austerity, forms of artistic expression like dance are one of the areas of public spending that is cut first, with many believing government funding should be targeted only at essential services. At a time when such government cuts to the arts take place, dance educators often find themselves unable to reach out to those who might most benefit from the cognitive, physical and social benefits that come from dance. The Internet has brought with it many opportunities for dance educators to provide access to their ideas on dance. For instance, YouTube allows for videos of dance lessons to be published, and MOOCs – Massively Open Online Courses – allow for high quality online lessons to be available to a wide number of people. However, such approaches are not the solution to increase access to dance education, as they are often non-participatory and difficult to translate into real-world practice. The solution is for dance educators to tap into social media to build interest in dance education, so people are willing to come to them privately with their own money, meaning the need for public funding is eliminated. This paper explores in depth the role of informal and immediate learning via social media – in this case Yahoo!Answers – in allowing dance educators to encourage those interested in dance to further that interest and not be put off by others prejudices, such as relating to prejudices around gender, sex and sexuality.

Sociological and cultural factors relating to dance education

For sociologists that study dance, a difficulty exists in that the sociology of culture can be considered to be inadequately served by sociology as a whole (Brinson 1983, 59-68). Indeed, the sociology of dance as a subdivision of the sociology of culture is seen to be closer to the European tradition of sociology than to the American one (Brinson 1983, 59-68). In South Korea the dance culture is also different, because when Korean dance teachers coach their students, they tend to address the group rather than individuals. Specifically, Korean teachers emphasize groups acting as one, and finding perfection in group performance (Berliner 2011, 15-17). In Denmark, where a fundamental idea is that "musical folk culture," it is put that a "master-apprentice" relationship is the path that should be taken (Aschengreen and Urup 1995, 73-75), which makes informal learning difficult to achieve.

At the European level in general, dance finds its way into meetings held under the auspices of anthropology and folk culture, meaning there are very few meetings with the discipline focus of dance itself (Lolacono 1994, 44-46; Grau 1995, 77-80). In addition, some have argued that dance can be seen as both a constructed medium of artistic practices, and not only as an expressed reflection of the broader redefining cultures that exist in society (De Spain 2000, 2-17). In North Africa, dance is usually associated with voluptuous movements of the torso, and also so integral a part of the folk culture that a "peasant" attempts to engage in without self-consciousness (Wood and Shay 1976, 18-30).

Types of "dance culture"

Understanding one's own culture and the culture of others is one thing that can be attained through dance, namely because culture is a fusion of thought and feeling (Allen 1988, 65-73; Patterson 1955, 421-430). It is thought that the existence of the global mass culture around dance is essentially centred in the West and that most forms of cultural representation tend to become homogenised, appearing manufactured (Foley 2001, 34-45). It has been argued that the dance as an art form as dissipated because the mass media is no longer interested in appealing to "high culture" and because a significant segment of the "art-loving" public is unaware of the existence of them (Van Dyke 2010, 208-230). Dances that are more culturally significant at present instead focus on the movements of the hips as a mean so as to engage the buttocks in a sexy, rhythmic, gyrating and shaking fashion, now termed by the mass media and others as 'twerking' (Richardson 2013, 327-341).

There is, however, a new counterculture emerging in dance, which is especially associated with music. The fusion experiments of music artists towards dance, along with more open-minded young audiences, means that progressive rock, jazz-rock, and jazz-funk are, to the dismay of purist critics, becoming more popular (Gaines 2013). This is not in itself new, if one considers the original counterculture of the 1960s. At this point in history, the creation of discotheques as nightclubs that featuring recorded music, created inspired customers with writhing "go-go girls" demonstrating new dance routines, including with some going topless (O'Neill 2011). Such practices are considered normal today and an accepted part of modern life, even though at the time they were seen as deviant.

Today's music and dance countercultures require a deeper understanding of artists, especially those Black males who often take up more authentic hip-hop spaces that are not provider for by institutionalised education (Irby, Petchauer, and Kirkland 2013, 15-36). This therefore requires a change in how dance education is conducted, which should perhaps include tolerance for both informal and immediate approaches to learning dance, including the creation of fun and fresh combos, dance routines and other training styles, based on improvisation and other instantaneous approaches to improve coordination between mind and matter.

Informal and immediate learning for dance education

Informal learning is the name given to a situation where knowledge transformation occurs outside a structured learning environment. That is not to say that informal learning has no place in education curricula, simply that it relies on the initiative of the learner to not want to be hoarded into a classroom and spoon-fed by a teacher. The 'flipped classroom' is one such approach to education, which encourages learners to do their homework in the class following making use of social media and other learning sources prior to attending. Immediate learning can often take the form of experiential learning, where learning goals of educators and learners can be met. Immediate learning and informal learning therefore can be seen to go hand-in-hand.

Both immediate and informal education can therefore have an important place in dance education more generally. The development of new abilities that have wide applicability, such as those that make use of autonomous and informal learning processes (Livingstone and Pankhurst 2009, 309-326), can be seen to be effectively formed through the aesthetic side of dance, including the use of music and drama, as well as the visual arts. Indeed, some dance educators are willing to acknowledge that so-called "dance culture" is not always synonymous with what those putting together curricula deem "culturally relevant," as it is often designed to accommodate local concerns (McCarthy-Brown 2009, 120-125). Despite this, there are dance educators who want to use dance instruction not only to reproduce the status quo, but to also try to change the way their learners see and engage with the wider world (Stinson 2005, 51-57).

By taking into account both local and global factors equally, providers of informal learning can bring together street theatre, music, dance, puppetry and poetry so as to create a fusion between the competing interests of their students and therefore stimulate discussion in a way that builds a collective commitment to change (Latchem 2014, 2015-21-01). Informal learning can therefore be utilised in environments where the teacher is willing to take less of a role, where the design of their sessions is about encouraging dance activity and not to focus on learning music as a theoretical subject (Folkestad 2005, 279-287; Folkestad 2006, 135-145).

Those who frequently participate in more informal and social forms of dance are known to be more likely to think about their so-called "free time" as being synonymous with their "dance time" (Hast 1993, 21-32). It could therefore be argued that informal learning is how such persons approach dance naturally, without any changes to the way they do this, unlike with the way dance is taught in institutionalised environments. Informal learning is therefore at its most effective when everyone engages in it "naturally," so much that its theoretical grounding in sociocultural practices and their social institutions goes unnoticed by them (Paradise and Rogoff 2009, 102-138). Whilst learning to dance has a clear aim and identifiable outcome, dancing instructors are not necessarily required to follow externally structured criteria in the way they teach it (Ajello and Belardi 2005, 73-86), meaning the introduction of informal learning need not be considered problematic.

An investigation into informal learning on Yahoo!Answers

It could be argued from the last section that informal learning has an important role to play in making dance education more responsive to the needs of learners. As a result, this section presents a study that explores informal learning for dance education online, namely its manifestation on Yahoo!Answers. This website allows users to ask questions and for other users to suggest answers to them, having over a million active users (Aharon et al. 2015, 1257-1262). Yahoo!Answers is one of the most renown question and answer websites (Zhou et al. 2015, 389-416), making it most likely to produce a good number of results relating to dance and dancing.

Methodology

The overall methodology for the study was based on a document analysis. Document analysis is known to be appropriate in qualitative studies, especially where it relates to policy development (Olsson et al. 2015, 72-82). Document analysis involves collecting relevant documents and records and coding them according to an agreed system (Kaya and Karamustafaoğlu 2015, 29-36). The documents in the study were selected through searching Yahoo!Answers for "dance" and "dancing" and to see what came up. Much of the study was phenomenological. That is, it required the researcher to be an instrument spotting trends, rather than using some mathematical formula to identify relevant postings, which might produce false positives. The codes and themes built from inspecting the data are in Table 1.

Table 1. Descriptions and codes of investigated categories

Category	Description	Codes
Gender, sex and sexuality issues	Sex is whether someone is a man or a woman, including whether they are a "boy" or "girl." Gender is whether someone is all or partly male or female. Sexual orientation is whether someone is attracted to the same sex, opposite sex, or both sexes. Sexuality is a combination of these to form a sexual identity.	Man, Woman, Gay / Homosexual, Bisexual, Straight
Race, citizenship, cultural issues, ethnicity	Someone's race includes whether for instance they are Caucasian, Afro-Caribbean, or similar. One's citizenship can be based on one's locality or nationality. Cultural issues include one's belief system, religion, values, etc. Ethnicity is a combination of all these to form an ethnic identity/	Skin/Colour, Black artist, local musician
Confidence issues	Confidence issues can include whether someone feels one is able to for instance sing and dance, how others might perceive one when singing or dancing. Essential, self-focussed and task-focussed anxiety. There is usually a need to overcome these issues.	I can't, I wish, how do I

Results

The selected documents were grouped according to a number of specific categories that became apparent to the research in inspecting the questions and answers. These included gender, sex and sexuality issues. Race, locality and cultural issues were also apparent, as were matters relating to confidence. After the articles were grouped according to these categories, they were then analysed in the context of the effect of the postings on whether they could be considered to amount to informal dance education. This was again based on the judgement of the researcher, who is an adult and community education worker, especially with regards to community arts. An example of such a community arts project is in Figure 1, where some of the same themes as in Table 1 came about as being the relevant concerns of the participants.

Figure 1: Young people representing race, citizenship and culture in a youth arts project.

Gender, sex and sexuality issues

Dance, as with most arts, has a situation where what is deemed feminine in one culture is considered masculine in another, albeit in some cases considered suitable for both sexes (Shay and Sellers-Young 2003, 13-37). The data showed this finding to be accurate. Consider a user called Man of God. They posted: "*Should all women learn the ancient art of belly dancing? I think your Man would appreciate it.*" Belly dancing is often perceived as a sexual dance in the West, but in reality it is nothing of the sort in Eastern cultures. Kollejira had her answer on belly dancing chosen by voters. "*Belly dancing isn't ancient, it's a modern style based on traditional types of dance, but with the 'hot factor' deliberately turned up a bit,*" the answer read. "*I do enjoy belly dancing, but there are no belly dancing classes near the area where I go to college, so I rarely get around to it, and when I do, I'm not very good at it.*"

These sexual associations are common among understandings of dance worldwide. They were present in the posts more generally, but most commonly in relation to women. "*Why do women like dancing? Is it sexual? Is it the closeness?*" is what Bucky asked. "*Every answer I have found is, 'It's fun.' Well why is it fun? I am not trying to cut down dance in any way and am not being macho,*" she continued. "*I just want to understand why so many women like dancing while so few men (myself included) do. Also, it seems to me that most men 'enjoy' dancing only as long as it can get them women. Since this is not my concern, why dance (sic) learn to dance at all?*"

To this question, Lady V responded:

> "*Most women like to dance because it's a form of expressing themselves in a joyous manner. It's one method of stress relieve (sic) in a positive, energetic way. Depending on the type of music, dancing can sometimes be meant for a sexual purpose of obtaining closeness to another individual. Dancing increases ones energy level, and boosts mental stamina. Yes,*

Dancing Is FUN! It has so many benefits, physical, mental, and social."

It might therefore be the case that the sexual associations with dance are as much about building confidence in oneself as artistic expression can in its own right. There is an enduring stereotype that male dancers – especially ballet dancers – are gay, whether in a homosexual or gender-bending way (Morrissey 2009). For instance, one user asked: "*Why are male ballet dancers considered 'gay' these days...? I'm starting ballet and I'm a teenager.*" A user called Adam said in response: "*I hope you are not gay. We could use a few non-gay ballet dancers. You know the women love you guys.*" Another user, Virginia, also commented. "*I danced classical ballet from a young age all through high school,*" she said. "*I was not gay and dated many ballet dancers during my time in different studios,*" she continued. "*I believe it is considered 'gay' because it does not present some form of macho competitiveness aspect,*" she concluded.

This can therefore show that not only does homophobia and sexism exist in informal learning on the subject of dance, but concerns about it often draw people to informal learning environments. This is because boys and men are generally expected to choose subjects like physical education over dance education (Gard 2001, 213-225). This would suggest that where appropriate guidance is given, informal learning can result in those interested in dance can be experientially motivated to take up further training. Equally, however, with the proliferation of homophobia, misogyny and indeed misandry, informal "*learning*" might result in less of a take-up of dance.

Race, locality and cultural issues

No matter how much experience one has of dance, knowing what is culturally acceptable can still be challenging (Siegel 1998, 91-97). Western and Eastern dance styles have historically developed in their respective countries on their own, with neither having a big influence on the other, but more recently as a result of globalisation, the conjugation between the Western and Eastern culture is a phenomenon that the dance world is experiencing to the fullest (Korman 2012, 22-32).

This global reach of different dance forms was evident from the data. One user, John was looking to learn hip hop dance, "*I have a lot of free time before I begin medical school so I figured hey, why not learn how to dance,*" he said. "*I've always been a fan of dancers such as Usher and Chis Brown but have no idea where to start. Any recommendations?*" he asked. "*I live in Dallas and there are a ton of hip hop dance studios around me. So if you guys recommend that, how should I go about picking the right one that is geared towards the style of dance I want to learn?*"

John was responded to by a user called Alair whose answer he chose as the one he agreed with. "*Prep yourself. You want to develop your own style, but you've got to get comfortable in your own skin before you start showing your moves,*" Alair said. "*Find an inspirational dancer in your neighborhood and ask if they'll teach you. Check at your local gym. Hip hop dancing is a great way to stay in shape, and it's fun, too,*" he added.

It is unclear whether John is trolling, or in other words being provocative. For instance, it is not clear whether or not his comments are meant as a joke. The reference by John that he is going to medical school might suggest he feels a sense of importance from this. By saying he wants to take-up dancing before this might in turn suggest he sees dancing as inferior.

Confidence issues

There are strong associations between people who have confidence issues and whether they decide to take up dancing. Young men who are interested in dancing often do so to attract women for friendship and love (Feely 2010, 90-110). Taking part in dance can also overcome the depression some might experience during their lives, but only for as long as they continue to take part in dance recitals (Vicario, Henninger, and Chambliss 2001).

Consider the called Razy, who was keen to start learning online. "So there's this competition in my college in October," she said. "Most of my friends are into dance and m (sic) really looking forward to taking part this year," she continued. "The problem is, I can't dance," they said prior to concluding: "Any tips for me and any links to help me out?" The best answer chosen by voters was "y dont u try online dance videos or youtube." This shows an inherent culture of informal learning in existence, where forms of social media like YouTube are seen as an appropriate reference source. Whereas in the past one may have had to buy a dance VHS or DVD recording, today one can find tips and instruction online. This allows for those interested in dancing to try things out without the expense of joining a club, or indeed buying video instructional materials in durable form. Fears of risks from the misuse or copyrighted or trademarked material can be alleviated with the use of corporate-owned platforms like YouTube, because corporations like Google will often ignore the rights of intellectual property holders, knowing that it would cost a lot in legal fees for them to be challenged personally as a mega corporation.

The costs of taking part in local dance club was a concern for some users. For instance, Brooke9920 asked, "*I'm taking a beginners (sic) ballet class next semester in college. I think it looks fun but, some people are trying to persuade me not to take it because it is really hard dance to learn. Is this true? Is ballet hard to learn? Why?*" The user chosen as best answer by Brooke9920 was JB who gave a 7 paragraph answer which started: "*DO NOT listen when people tell you not to take something, it is not their choice. If you would like to take a ballet class, then by all means do, I would.*" Brooke9920's response was, "*Thank you so much! Your answer was excellent. I'm sticking with ballet!*"

This shows that informal learning environments like Yahoo!Answers can provide social support to encourage others to do things such as dance. In another case, Naomi posted a question asking: *"I'm 20 years old turning 21 in 6 months, and was just curious if I would be too old to learn to dance? LIke hip hop or anything like that."* The answer by Rahul who was chosen by voters was: *"If in reasonably good health, you are probably never too old to start; but I speak mostly of ballroom dancing... I know little to nothing about 'modern' dancing. This forum's primary focus is ballroom, but there may well be someone here with experience in Modern who can respond in a more helpful way."*

This concern has some relevance in the literature. It has been shown that confidence can be seriously damaged through taking part in ballroom dances, often because it is more physical and the sexual aspects of it can feel immoral to those who are in a romantic relationship at the same time as dancing with other people (Ashley 2012, 25-33). Taking part in dance could be seen as an opportunity for someone to improve confidence in other areas of their life. Equally, however, the more complex dancing becomes, its impact on confidence could be damaged by those without the experience of dancing at a more advanced level. Informal learning is therefore a double-edged sword that could either encourage or discourage participation in mainstream dance education, depending on how a potential dancer would perceive how others might see them. Yahoo!Answers might therefore be better served if those that take part in dance signed up and provided more authentic and realistic answers, in the way those without genuine expertise in dance would fail to provide.

Discussion

This paper has investigated the existence of informal learning opportunities in social media as far as it related to dance education. The paper has sought to show how interest in formal dance education can be increased through dance educators providing informal learning via social media. It is argued that by dance educators participating in question and answer websites such as Yahoo!Answers, they can increase interest in formal dance education, and help those who might be interested in paying for dance education to overcome any fears they might have, including prejudice from others.

It found a number of issues and prejudices that exist in the way dance is presented online, which could limit the effectiveness of informal learning. Confidence issues play a big role in how informal education may affect choices to take up dance education opportunities, and so even informal learning needs to prevent such confidence being damaged. Through investigating Yahoo!Answers – by treating it as an informal learning provider - a number of findings that are relevant to dance education as a whole were made. The platform often had answers that were sincere, although it was also possible "trolling" existed among them. That is, many questions and answers were clearly not intended to be taken as serious solutions. Supportive answers included suggesting use of video platforms like YouTube to learn dancing. This further shows that social media, if one knows how to access it, can be ideal places for informal learning, outside the structures of traditional education institutions. This means that social media can be seen to be putting more opportunity into the hands of those who might not have confidence to take up traditional programmes of study.

In addition, novel approaches to learning, such as the 'flipped classroom,' can involve using informal learning prior to classroom attendance. For instance, dance students could be asked to look at videos on YouTube that are of interest to them and then reflect on these in the classroom. Dance workshops need not be based solely on the demonstration approach, but can become student-centred by integrating informal learning into the curriculum. In practical subjects like dance, each person will have their own aims and objectives when attending formal learning environments. On this basis, encouraging greater use of informal learning can form an important part of the process of reflection. Through exploring students' informal learning, it is much easier for educators or training to building on the existing knowledge of learners, rather than expecting them to adopt approaches that might go against the grain. The paper has suggested that if experts in dance were to make use of platforms like Yahoo!Answers then there can be a wider benefit of greater take-up of formal dance education, if such experts can give those asking questions about dance to be more confident in taking it up.

References

Aharon, M., A. Kagian, Y. Kaplan, R. Nissim, and O. Somekh (2015). Serving ads to yahoo answers occasional visitors.International World Wide Web Conferences Steering Committee, .

Ajello, A.M. and C. Belardi (2005). Making non-formal and informal learning visible through digital portfolios. In Trading up: Potential and performance in non-formal learning, eds. Chisholm, Hoskins and C. Glahn, 73-86. Strasbourg, FR: Council of Europe.

Allen, B. (1988). Teaching training and discipline-based dance education. Journal of Physical Education, Recreation & Dance 59(9), 65-73.

Aschengreen, E. and H. Urup. (1995). Dance research in denmark. Dance Research Journal 27(1), 73-75.

Ashley, L. (2012). Folk dance a survival story. In Dancing with difference, ed. L. Ashley, 25-33. Berlin, DE: Springer.

Berliner, L. (2011). A collaborative process under the spanish sun. Dance Major Journal 2011(Spring), 15-17.

Brinson, P. (1983). Scholastic tasks of a sociology of dance: Part 2. Dance Research: The Journal of the Society for Dance Research 1(2), 59-68.

De Spain, K. (2000). Dance and technology: A pas de deux for post-humans. Dance Research Journal 32(1), 2-17.

Feely, C. (2010). From dialectics to dancing: Reading, writing and the experience of everyday life in the diaries of frank P. forster. 69(1):90-110.

Foley, C. (2001). Perceptions of irish step dance: National, global, and local. Dance Research Journal 33(1), 34-45.

Folkestad, G. (2006). Formal and informal learning situations or practices vs formal and informal ways of learning. British Journal of Music Education 23(2), 135-145.

Folkestad, G. (2005). Here, there and everywhere: Music education research in a globalised world. Music Education Research 7(3), 279-287.

Gaines, K. (2013). Birds of fire: Jazz, rock, funk, and the creation of fusion by kevin fellezs. Durham, NC: Duke University Press.

Gard, M. (2001). Dancing around the 'problem' of boys and dance. Discourse 22(2), 213-225.

Grau, A. (1995). Dance research in the United Kingdom. Dance Research Journal 27(2), 77-80.

Hast, D.E. (1993). Performance, transformation, and community: Contra dance in new england. Dance Research Journal 25(1), 21-32.

Irby, D.J., E. Petchauer, and D. Kirkland. (2013). Engaging black males on their own terms: What schools can learn from black males who produce hip-hop. Multicultural Learning and Teaching 8(2), 15-36.

Kaya, M. and O. Karamustafaoğlu. (2015). Analysis of TSKT questions on science teaching in 2013 PPSS according to reconstructing of bloom taxonomy. Eurasian Journal of Physics and Chemistry Education 7(1), 29-36.

Korman, S. (2012). East meets west. Journal of Physical Education, Recreation & Dance 83(1), 22-32.

Latchem, C.R. (2014). Informal learning and non-formal education for development. Journal of Learning for Development 1 (1):2015-21-01. http://www.jl4d.org/index.php/ejl4d/article/view/6.

Livingstone, D.W. and K.V. Pankhurst. (2009). Education and jobs: The way ahead. In Education and jobs: Exploring the gaps, ed. D.W. Livingstone, 309-326. Toronto, CA: University of Toronto Press.

Lolacono, D.C. (1994). Dance research in the United Kingdom. Dance Research Journal 26(1), 44-46.

McCarthy-Brown, N. (2009). The need for culturally relevant dance education. Journal of Dance Education 9(4):120-125.

Morrissey, S.A. (2009). Dancing Around Masculinity?: Young Men Negotiating Risk in the Context of Dance Education. PhD, University of Aberdeen.

Olsson, L., L. Hjalmarsson, M. Wikström, and M. Larsson. (2015). Bridging the implementation gap: Combining backcasting and policy analysis to study renewable energy in urban road transport. Transport Policy 37, 72-82.

O'Neill, W.L. (2011). Dawning of the counter-culture Now and Then Reader LLC.

Paradise, R. and B. Rogoff. (2009). Side by side: Learning by observing and pitching in. Ethos 37(1), 102-138.

Patterson, A.D. (1955). The "new look" in student teaching. The Educational Forum 19(4), 421-430.

Richardson, E. (2013). Developing critical hip hop feminist literacies: Centrality and subversion of sexuality in the lives of black girls. Equity & Excellence in Education 46(3), 327-341.

Risner, D. (2010). Dance education matters: Rebuilding postsecondary dance education for twenty-first century relevance and resonance. Journal of Dance Education 10(4), 95-110.

Shay, A. and B. Sellers-Young. (2003). Belly dance: Orientalism: Exoticism: Self-exoticism. Dance Research Journal 35(1), 13-37.

Siegel, M.B. (1998). Bridging the critical distance. In The routledge dance studies reader, eds. A. Carter and J. O'Shea. Second ed., 91-97. Abingdon, GB: Routledge.

Stinson, S.W. (2005). The hidden curriculum of gender in dance education. Journal of Dance Education 5(2), 51-57.

Van Dyke, J. (2010). Vanishing: Dance audiences in the postmodern age. Dance Chronicle 33(2), 208-230.

Vicario, T., E. Henninger, and C. Chambliss. (2001). The Correlates of Dance Education among Adolescent Girls: ERIC.

Wood, L. and A. Shay. (1976). Danse du ventre: A fresh appraisal. Dance Research Journal 8(2), 18-30.

Zhou, T.C., M.R. Lyu, I. King, and J. Lou. (2015). Learning to suggest questions in social media. Knowledge and Information Systems 43(2), 389-416.

Citizen Journalism Practice in Nigeria: Trends, Concerns, and Believability

Joseph Wilson and Fancis Iloani Arinze

Abstract: Journalism practice globally in the last two decades has experienced some obvious changes. For instance, it is no longer the case that the business of gathering, processing and distribution of information, which for several decades was supposedly a preserve of practitioners that have acquired some form of training in the field of journalism and are guided by journalism ethos or ethics. With societal development and technological advancement, individuals have delved into exercising the functions of journalists, which has led to the emergence of concepts such as "Citizen Journalism" among others. The emergence of citizen journalism obviously has its plus in the rapid development of the information society, with the active participation of members of the society processing information. However, there are several concerns. Since journalism now seems to be an all-comers affair, obviously there are bound to be deficiencies in strictly upholding the tenets of Journalism profession such as truthfulness, accuracy, objectivity, impartiality, fairness, authentication of sources and public accountability. This chapter explores the nature of citizen journalism as practiced in Nigeria, the channels that propel citizen journalism practice in Nigeria, the concerns in respect to ethos or ethics and whether Nigerians believe the products of this new form of journalism (things posted online) and why.

Keywords: Political participation; Social media; Political websites; Facebook; Nigeria; ICTs; Online forums.

Introduction

The media landscape has tremendously changed in recent times in ways that make it possible for a more engaged citizen participation in journalism. Citizens now exercise the functions of gathering, processing and dissemination of information; a phenomenon widely known as citizen Journalism.

The emergence of citizen journalism has obviously contributed to the rapid development of the information society, with the active participation of members of the society in processing information (Oak, 2011). In a country like Nigeria with a population of over 150 million, it would be of interest to know how Nigeria with its diversity fares in respect of citizens' participation in the information society. Since Journalism now seems an all comers affair irrespective of a participant's status, spurred on by the availability/affordability of new media technologies in Nigeria and bearing in mind that Nigeria due to its history of prolonged military leadership, which even though now in a democratic system, hitherto still exhibits the exclusivity and secrecy of the past military order plus speculative journalism , rumour and information fabrication taking a centre stage (Nnamani, 2003), what is the nature of this newly found form of Journalism (Citizen Journalism) in Nigeria? What are the concerns in citizen journalism in Nigeria? What is the status of the ethical principles of truthfulness, accuracy, objectivity, impartiality, fairness, authentication of sources and public accountability, among others? Do Nigerians believe the "products" of this form of journalism and why?

This paper attempts to provide answers to these questions and looks at citizen journalism practice in Nigeria with the following objectives: to identify channels of this participatory journalism in Nigeria, to look at the trend or nature of practice, to identify concerns in citizen journalism practice in Nigeria as it relates to ethos and to identify whether people believe the things they see posted online and why.

Citizen Journalism is a concept that has generated argument in respect of its appropriateness of the use of the concept, its definition, its channels, and who are those involved, among others. According to Meyer (1995) one measure of the discomfort that journalists feel over the concept of participatory journalism is the great variety of names given it, e.g. civic journalism, citizen journalism, community journalism, or communitarian journalism. It is as though all who try some version of it want to distance themselves from the questionable practices of the others and that each sees in it the manifestation of his or her fondest hopes or worst fears (ibid).

It might seem difficult to have a clear-cut definition of the citizen journalism concept at the moment and the argument may rage on, but what is important is the understanding that participatory form of journalism exist. A form of journalism that gives individual or groups in the society the opportunity to participate in reporting events, opinion and occurrences using various channels. Banda (2010) notes that, whilst there are various perspectives on what constitutes citizen journalism, the underlying concept of citizen engagement in newsgathering, processing and distribution remain the central focus.

Gillmor (2006) provides a broader clarification on the concept of citizen journalism based on the various technologies involved. Gillmor notes that citizen journalism has been spurred on by the growth in the availability of the new-media platforms of desktop publishing and other technologies that have come to characterize citizen journalism, like those in Table 1.

The practice that enables individuals participate in news reportage is what is today referred to as citizen journalism (Rogers, 2011). Gaulin (2007) notes that Citizen journalism, also sometimes referred to broadly as user-generated content, is when anyone can participate in the gathering, writing, reporting, and even the publishing of news. Citizen journalism can be published on a site like associated content, on a blog, or any other avenue online. Citizen journalism is a way for everyone to be involved in the media, and of fulfilling what Rogers, (2011), describes as their freedom of expression.

Table 1. Publishing platforms and technologies

Information factor	Description
Mail lists and forums	Made up of diverse communities of interest
Weblogs	A 'many to many, few to few' medium whose 'ecosystem' is 'expanding into the space between email and the Web
Wikis	Server programmes that allow users to collaborate in forming the content of a Web site
SMSs	A service offered by network providers which allows customers to send text messages over the cell phones
Mobile-connected cameras	Includes the every-day digital cameras that allow users to download, store, edit, and transmit pictures anytime, anywhere
Internet 'broadcasting'	Whereby ordinary people can record and upload anything on to the Internet, as well as distribute it
Peer-to-peer (P2P)	Sharing of files
RSS (Really Simple Syndication)	Allows readers of blogs and other kinds of sites to have their computers and other devices automatically retrieve the content they care about.

Citizen journalism, also known as participatory journalism, is the act of citizens playing an active role in the process of collecting, reporting, analysing and disseminating news and information. It is the concept of members of the public playing an active role in the process of collecting, reporting, analysing and disseminating news and information. The intent of this participation is to provide independent, wide-ranging and relevant information that a democracy requires (Bowman and Willis, 2003). Rogers (2011) notes that citizen journalism is when private individuals do essentially what professional journalists or reporters do – source and report information which takes many forms, from a podcast editorial to a report about a city council meeting on a blog.

Table 2. Types of media for citizen journalism

Type	Examples
Audience participation	User comments attached to news stories, personal blogs, photos or video footage captured from personal mobile cameras, or local news written by residents of a community.
Independent news and information Websites	Consumer Reports, the Drudge Report
Full-fledged participatory news sites	Sahara reporters, NowPublic, OhmyNews, DigitalJournal.com, GroundReport
Collaborative and contributory media sites	Slashdot, Kuro5hin, Newsvine
Other kinds of "thin media."	Mailing lists, email newsletters
Personal broadcasting sites	Video broadcast sites such as KenRadio
"One mobile phone to many"	Citizen Journalism

It can include text, pictures, audio and video. But it is about communicating information of some kind. This practice was largely enhanced by the emergence of the Internet, mobile phone and other ICT - with blogs, podcasts, streaming video and other Web-related innovations - that have made citizen journalism possible. Similarly, Flew (2008) states that there are three elements critical to the rise of citizen journalism and citizen media: open publishing, collaborative editing and distributed content. Lasica (2003) classified media for citizen journalism into various types shown in Table 2.

Another common form of citizen journalism is "one mobile phone to many". This classification of citizen journalism entails an individual using mobile phone to disseminate text messages, multimedia messages to as many contacts available to the sender. Rogers (2011) further categorized citizen journalism into two forms: Semi-independent citizen journalism and Independent citizen journalism.

Semi-Independent Citizen Journalism

This has to do with citizens contributing, in one form or another, to existing professional news sites. In this case readers post their comments alongside news stories written by professional reporters – what Rogers (2011) described as essentially a 21st-century version of the letter to the editor. A growing number of news websites such as Sahara Reporters, Premium Times, Next and all Nigerian online newspapers allow readers to post comments and sometimes give updates and opinion about a news item or report. In most cases many websites require users to register to make such posts. In this regard, Rogers (2011) notes that, it is an effort to prevent obscene or objectionable messages, many websites require that readers register in order to post comments.

There are several news stories on issues of national interest have attracted a lot of posts from Nigerians, using various platforms. For example, post-election violence in Kaduna State of Nigeria in 2011. When the story appeared online, readers posted information about the post-election violence in areas not covered in the breaking news. The posts/comment also provided details on the role of the police during the post-election incidence. Another example is the recent abduction of over 200 schoolgirls in Chibok-Nigeria. Citizens have often sent contributions to mainstream media organizations on developments on the abduction. Such information is sometimes incorporated into the final news story that is sent out to the audience by such media organizations.

Independent Citizen Journalism: This involves citizen journalists working in ways that are fully independent of traditional, professional news outlets. For example, blogs in which individuals can report on events in their communities or offer commentary on current issues. Franklin Avenue, Nairaland, Nigeroiabloggers.com are some examples independent citizen journalism. There are also hybrid sites such as Bluffton Today Ohmynews, in which professional and citizen journalists work together.

The independent citizen journalism also includes websites operated by an individual or a group of people that report on news events in the local community. Some have editors and screen content, others do not. Some even have print editions. Examples: Sahara Reporters, Daily Heights, iBrattleboro.

Glaser (2006) points out that the idea behind citizen journalism is "that people without professional journalism training can use the tools of modern technology and the global distribution of the Internet to create, augment or fact-check media on their own or in collaboration with others," adding that one "might snap a digital photo of a newsworthy event happening in your town and post it online," finally suggesting that one "might videotape a similar event and post it on a site such as YouTube."

For the purpose of conceptual clarification this paper adopts the definition of citizen Journalism as journalism practice that involves individual or group participation in gathering, processing dissemination information through several channels.

It is common in recent times to watch video footages, pictures, read and listen to reports of news event on several web pages, blogs and social media such as the Facebook, YouTube, twitter, and the websites of international mainstream media stations such as British Broadcasting Corporation (BBC), Voice of America (VOA), Cable News Network (CNN), Radio France International (RFI) Deutche Welle Radio, etc. sent by amateurs or eye witnesses and are disseminated worldwide. For example, in August, 2006 CNN launched CNN EXCHANGE, a page that encourages visitors to submit their stories, pictures and videos in order to enrich the professional 24/7 news coverage provided by CNN. Recent conflicts in the Middle East brought about a massive submission of stories, pictures and videos on blogs, online picture and video repositories around the web. In line with this, CNN and other international media decided to open their doors to such submissions to enrich their own news coverage and keep their audience on their pages.

Edmonds (2011) notes that citizens armed with cell phones or other digital-cameras, can be counted on to enhanced coverage of news worthy events. For example, events like the tsunami, Hurricane Katrina, the New York twin tower tragedy, the Arab Spring, Nigeria 2011 general election and the post-election violence, the occupy Nigeria removal of petrol subsidy street protest etc., got various forms of coverage from members of the public through still photos and streaming videos which in some cases were used by media giants such as BBC and CNN. Blog reports also provide an unmediated, ground-level view on huge stories like September 11 world trade centre tragedy, and most recently the Middle East uprising, the Nigeria post-election violence May 2011 and the occupy Nigeria

January 2012 fuel subsidy removal protest. Edmonds further notes that traditional media are now indulging in getting urgent about bringing blogs or citizen-written sites into their mix.

In line with Edmond's position, Rogers (2011) also points out, that the Egyptian uprising that led to the resignation of president Hosni Mubarak besides being historic in the politics of the Middle East, it was also a story about journalism – how citizens among other journalistic efforts, played a role in spreading word of the revolution and sent video footages to conventional media establishments.

Emergence and Development of Citizen Journalism

The notion of citizens' participation in the act of journalism has a long history in the developed countries like the United States. Glaser (2006), notes that the earliest form of citizen journalism is traced to the founding of the United States in the 18th century, when pamphleteers such as Thomas Paine and the anonymous authors of the Federalist Papers gained prominence by printing their own publications. In the modern era, video footage of the assassination of President John F. Kennedy in the '60s and footage of police beating Rodney King in Los Angeles in the '80s were both captured by citizens on the scene of the event, the rise of talk radio and the styling of cable access television gave people the opportunity to share their views and news stories with a much larger audience.

In newspapers, there were letters to the editor submitted by citizens, while pirate radio stations hit the airwaves without the permission of the regulation agencies, for example in Nigeria stations like Radio NADECO, Radio Kudirat, Voice of free Nigeria and Radio Voice of Biafra International were used during the military administrations in Nigeria by those opposed to military regimes. The advent of desktop publishing in the late 1980s allowed a lot of people to design and print out their own publications, but distribution was still limited. The unprecedented rise and penetration of the World Wide Web technology in the 1990s, made it possible for several people to set up a personal home page to share their thoughts with the world.

An important milestone in the history of citizen journalism was when journalists themselves began to question the predictability of their coverage of such events as the 1988 U.S. presidential election. Those journalists became part of the public, or civic, journalism movement, a countermeasure against the eroding trust in the news media and widespread public disillusionment with politics and civic affairs (Meyer, 1995; Merritt, 2004; Dvorkin, 2005). Others include eyewitness bloggers in Iraq such as Salam Pax giving stunningly detailed early accounts of the war. The 2004 U.S. political conventions, bloggers were given press passes for the first time. In 2005, ordinary citizens with their camera phones took the earliest photos on the scene of the London bombings on July 7. The pictures and videos of 2011 post-election violence in some parts of Northern Nigeria uploaded by individuals on YouTube, Facebook and other social networking sites. Mainstream media sites run by the BBC accepted photos, video and text reports -- a practice that continues to this day among many major broadcast organizations (Gaser, 2006).

What became known as citizen journalism is the result of the digital era's democratization of media - wide access to powerful, inexpensive tools of media creation; and wide access to what people created, via digital networks - after a long stretch when manufacturing-like mass media prevailed. Blogging was one of the first major tools in this genre (Gillmor, 2008).

Observably, Citizen Journalism began to develop, spurred by emerging internet and networking technologies, such as, chat rooms and weblogs. Then came the use of convergent polls, allowing editorials and opinions to be submitted and voted on. Gillmor (2008) notes that as to whom citizen journalism concept was first affiliated to in its current digital-age meaning is Oh Yeon Ho, founder of Korea's OhmyNews, who said that "Every citizen is a reporter. The South Korea based, OhmyNews started in year 2000 and became popular and commercially successful with the motto, "Every Citizen is a Reporter. It operates with about 40 traditional reporters and editors who write about 20% of its content, with the rest coming from other freelance contributors who are mostly ordinary citizens. OhmyNews now has an estimated 50,000 contributors, and has been credited with transforming South Korea's conservative political environment. Today the concept is used globally and the practice is everywhere.

Nigerian Context

Citizen journalism in Nigeria like other countries of the world is an old practice, in the sense that audience long before the penetration of new communication technologies had ways of interacting with the conventional media. However, the unprecedented involvement of citizens in reporting events and disseminating information has been greatly enhanced by the development in ICT. When Nigeria opened up its shores to information technologies and even came up with information technology policy to enhance and promote the use of technology for development generally in the late 1990 and the beginning of the new millennium, the country witnessed an unprecedented ICT penetration which has today placed it among the leading subscribers of technology like the mobile phone. The rise of internet cafes across the country and the floating of several telecommunication networks and services afforded Nigerians the opportunity to engage in massive gathering and dissemination of all sorts of information through the internet and mobile phones.

Banda (2010) adds that in Nigeria, citizen journalism is a growing phenomenon and traditional media organizations as well as individuals and non-governmental organizations are supporting this growth. Olubunmi et al. (2011) note that recent national and international developments are demonstrating the power of technology to transform communication channels, media sources, events, and the fundamental nature of journalism. Technological advances now allow citizens to record and instantly publicize information and images for immediate distribution on ubiquitous communication networks using social media such as Twitter, Facebook, and YouTube. These technologies are enabling non-journalists to become "citizen reporters" (also known as "citizen journalists"), who record and report information over informal networks or via traditional mass media channels

According to Kperogi (2011), two momentous developments have occurred in the Nigerian journalistic landscape in the last ten years which include the migration of all major Nigerian newspapers to the Internet and the robust growth and flowering of diasporan online news outlets that have actively sought and captured the attention and participation of readers.

With these developments, the trend and channels of citizen journalism in Nigeria now became obvious. Weblogs, made in or by Nigerian began to emerge and the international media like the BBC, VOA, Radio France International, Deutsche Welle Radio also provided avenues for Nigerians to post, and make calls and report event during broadcast hours. Popular news sites like the Sahara Reporters,Nairaland.com, Nigerian Plus, Nigeria village Squire, Point blank news, Huhuonline.com, Nigeria Plus Nigerian Best Forum, Webtrends Nigeria, Nigeria Plus , citizen journalism association of Nigeria, etc. are some indigenous sites that give Nigerians opportunity to practice the form(s) of citizen journalism as categorized earlier.

These sites enable citizens send reports, comments and views on various issues affecting Nigeria and beyond. Nigerian newspapers if not all, almost all have online versions which also avails citizens the opportunity to make comments on issues covered by the online newspapers.

Observation has shown that one of the widely patronized channels are the international radio stations that promote some form of citizen journalism by allowing citizens to phone in during broadcast and report on issues. For example, the 2011 Nigeria general election witnessed a display of citizens' contribution to the broadcast items by the international media.

The Social media are also not left out especially among the Information technology literates. The popular networking site, the Facebook, YouTube, Twitter, MySpace, also provide another popular avenue for Nigerians to post information as a form of citizen journalism practice.

A recent trend in citizen journalism is the emergence of online news sites inviting contributions from local residents of their subscription areas, who often report on topics that conventional newspapers tend to ignore. According to Glaser (2004), citizen participation in journalism has changed the conventional journalism practice. Instead of being the gatekeeper, telling people what is important to them, the public now serving as the eyes and ears for the Voice, rather than having everything filtered through the views of a small group of reporters and editors.

Theoretical Discussion

Patterson (2008) notes that since the days of ancient Greek, philosophers have tried to draft series of guidelines concerning ethical issues. There are contributions by scholars in the area of media ethics, some of which appear suitable to explaining ethos in citizen journalism. Some of these contributors include Aristotle's Golden Mean theory; Immanuel Kant's categorical imperative theory; Jeremy Banthem and John Staurt Mill's Utilitarianism; Pluralistic theory of value; and communitarianism. There is also the Media Ethics theory widely referred to as the four normative media ethics theory. This paper touches on a few of these theories as framework to further explain ethos in citizen journalism. The paper adopts Aristotle Golden theory, categorical imperative theory, communitarianism and the social responsibility theories as framework.

The Aristotle Golden Mean theory from the Nichmachean Ethics stipulates that one way to learn ethics is to select heroes and to try to model your individual acts and ultimately your professional character on what you believe they would do. That means this theory is about the proper emotional response to situation, rather than the proper action. That virtue come from character and character make one do the right thing (Murdarasi, 2008). This explains the need for a citizen journalist to model their practice after experts or professional in the field of journalism to ensure that contributions or reports should be ethos based.

The Immanuel Kent categorical imperatives asserts that an individual should act on the premise that choices one make for oneself could become universal law therefore one should act so that humanity is treated always as an end never as a means only. Kent asserts that there are certain things one always had a duty to always do irrespective of consequences of doing them. For example, he believes people should always tell the truth and it is important to find out what one's moral duties are, achieved through reasoning (Patterson, 2008 and Guthrie 1994). Based on this theory, Patterson (2008) notes that, for instance an ethical person drive at a speed and in a manner that is appropriate to everyone else on the same highway. Patterson further notes that journalist can claim few special privileges, such as the right to lie or invade privacy in order to get a story, Kent view however remind one of what one gives up: truth and privacy. Citizen journalist may not have code of ethics but reasoning along Kent theory would help practitioners avoid ethical blunders.

Communitarianism theory places its dominant intellectual emphasis on individual and individual acts by emphasizing concepts such as character, choice, liberty and duty. Communitarian thinking allows ethical discussions to include value such as altruism. According to Turner (2006) Communitarianism emerged in the 1980s as a response by Charles Taylor, Michael Sandel, and Michael Walze to the limits of liberal theory and practice. Its dominant themes are that individual rights need to be balanced with social responsibilities, and that autonomous selves do not exist in isolation, but are shaped by the values and culture of communities. Ethos in Citizen Journalism could fit in this context when citizen understand that certain responsibilities are expected of them based on community value.

Another theory relevant to this paper is Social Responsibility theory or media typology which McQuail (2000) postulates as: (1) media has obligation to society, (2) media ownership is a public trust, (3) news media should be should be truthful, accurate, fair, objective and relevant (4) media should be free but self-regulated, (5) media should follow agreed codes of ethics and professional conduct, (6) Under some circumstance, government may need to intervene to safeguard the public.

MCQuail further notes that the right of the people to have an adequate press and their rights taking precedence are fundamental bases for the demand for responsibility. Citizen journalism is a platform for individuals and groups to own or freely access means and freely disseminates information of their choices to the society. This freedom however requires certain level of responsibility and some touch of ethical standard, which Mgulwa (2008) points out that it should set guidelines, rules, norms, codes and principles that will lead journalists and all other media workers to make moral decisions. They should not be forced to do so because ethics is applied voluntarily. The emergence of new media such as the internet and mobile phone have transformed the conventional journalism, making it open for non-professionals which is creating challenges such as non-adherence to ethos of the profession.

Trend and Channels of Citizen Journalism in Nigeria

In the wake of emerging technologies and new digital tools, the Nigeria journalism landscape is changing rapidly especially with the online presence of most media organization: both electronic and print. Making them more interactive and dynamic and in some cases provide pictorial and video support. Online editions of newspapers now offer readers the option to comment on their content and share links on various social networks. They also feature embedded videos, blogs and the concept of mobile applications including SMS alerts of breaking news on mobile phones which is now a common phenomenon in Nigeria Journalism business.

The digital transformation is gradual but an obvious trend in Nigeria Citizen journalism is the utilization of social media and foreign conventional media channels (radio and television stations) to carry out their citizen journalism practice. For example, activities like webcasting - broadcasting live audio or video online – are popular channels in modern citizen journalism but observation has shown that the trend in Nigeria citizen journalism is the reliance on social media and foreign media channels to enjoy most of these services. For example the Facebook, Twitter, YouTube, British Broadcasting Corporation (BBC) World Service especially the Hausa service, Voice of America (VOA), Radio France International, Deutsche Welle Radio, Aljazera TV etc. are channels utilized by Nigerians to post and report news stories.

The disturbing trend as regards these channels is the often uncensored and unedited reports which have little or no regards for media ethos or ethics and neither do such reports and videos display any sense of social responsibility. For example, the spate of violence that trailed the Presidential polls in Nigeria in April 2011 and the current security challenges the country is facing. Nigerian citizens from various parts of the country covered the crises and still share information on the current security situation. For example, on Facebook a Nigerian resident in the United States posted a picture of a young man lying dead in pool of blood with machete wounds and it was tagged "body of a Youth Corps member murdered in Bauchi" (Bauchi is one of Nigeria's Northern States) A disturbing video was uploaded on YouTube, of a man set ablaze and it was tagged "post-election violence in Jos". The Social media are readily available channels for citizens and thus it comes handy for spreading distorted information. The insurgence and the recent abduction of schoolgirls in Chibok, Nigeria are constantly reported on various social media and other online platforms.

Social Media

Social media has an obvious place in citizen journalism practice in Nigeria. These media and other technologies shape the concept of citizen journalism. They make it easier and enable more people to participate in citizen journalism. The internet, mobile phones and affordable digital cameras have made the promotion of citizen journalism practice possible. Tools such as Twitter, Facebook and YouTube are widely used in citizen journalism practice in Nigeria. Banda (2010) notes that these technologies and media have in some instances determine shape of citizen journalism in Nigeria. Citizen journalists use social media platforms to disseminate news, comment and views on issues of national and international issues.

Nigerians have witnessed the power of the social media, with the presence of myriads of platform to share information gathered. Social sites like Facebook and Twitter and YouTube, present a platform for individuals to share information and expression of ideas (Samson, 2011)

For example, during the 2011 general elections, Nigerians went out ready to vote and monitor the process. They freely took pictures and shared them with friends and strangers alike. Samson (2011) notes that Daily Trust which has a wide followership on social sites became like a sub platform for the expression of opinion and the sharing of news with ordinary citizens sending in reports and photos from their various localities. Samson (2011) identified some of the messages sent via mobile phones, Facebook and Twitter, which can be seen below.

With respect to mobile phones:

"Accreditation has finished and voters have started queeing for voting. We have witness a serious low turnout in almost all the poling units in my home town Gashu'a" Adamu Kaku Gashu'a (+2348066014###).

"At kpansia 7 here in Yenagoa peoples cast as many as they like a friend of mind said he votes six times", Usman Adamu Yenagoa (+2348034011###).

On Facebook, many people posted regular updates the crisis:

Sanusi Altine, "I have just been disenfranchised by INEC in my poling unit together with tens of other people."

Somson (2011) further notes that with news travelling so fast with no gatekeeper, especially with the protection of anonymity, it then poses a potential risk as people with ulterior motives can abuse it to ferment trouble. "People just disseminate whatever comes to their mind without consideration of implication, supporting them with damning pictures in some cases," they said. "This is no little matter as a single malicious tweet of Facebook can make the rounds and reach hundreds of thousands in a short time, creating a storm in its wake," they concluded.

Otufodunrin (2012) posits that, the social media provide an opportunity for non-journalists to report events from their own perspective. Keita (2012) points out that in the race for relevancy, big players in the print media used Twitter to invite citizen reporters to contribute reporting. For example, Nigeria Vanguard newspaper on January 10 2012 tweeted in respect of a national strike in Nigeria:

"As Labour strike begins... report protest in your area!"

According to Olakitan (2012), the Internet has "given room to a new form of media freedom in information dissemination that has not been seen some few years ago." They argued that Nigerians are able to post information faster than an average journalist could send an article for production. "The recent mass protests of the oil subsidy removal in Nigeria had many users of twitters sharing pictures of dead or dying protesters," they said. "Many Nigerians entered into meaningful discussions on the subjects of corruption, police brutality, comparing figures and statistics on Facebook and posting comments," they concluded.

Many Nigerians covered the protests themselves through social media tools. Nigerians rarely rely on government owned media such as the National Television Authority, NTA and federal radio corporation that often broadcasts content in favour of the government. It is common scenario, in recent times for Nigerians to post their own videos on You Tube and inform friends on Facebook, Twitter or Skype. When incidences happen such as police or security agencies brutality are denied by offenders, eye witnesses do not hesitate to post pictures of such incidences or, pictures of the horror were posted on You Tube for all to see.

"The beauty of social media is that I control the information I want people to hear. I won't let people listen to lies from government," twitted @ekekeee. However, Adebanjo a professional journalist, points out that citizen reporting should be carried out with caution *"Please use Social Media responsibly and only broadcast what you have confirmed."*

Idowu (2012) notes, *"Social media have been helpful in mobilising public opinion against an unpopular public policy. But it is also a threat to responsible information dissemination. Unverified claims, outright lies have been dished almost in equal measure in the determination to coaltar the government and its officials."*

The use of SMS is another trend though unconventional but has a wide reach and often disturbing. As millions of Nigeria mobile phone subscribers can beached in matter of minutes. Report whether false news, fact distorted or truth, gets to the mobile phone of Nigerians at the fastest possible time. It is considered faster than the widely used social media and radio channels, recent text message that that circulated all over Nigeria by an unknown source drew the attention of the Nigerian Police to assure Nigerians that the text was baseless and untrue. The text was a warning to Christians living in the North to leave as there was Jihad planned to eliminate Christians house to house. A similar text was circulated among Muslims living in the North some times in 2011 that Muslims living in the south would be attacked. Another one was the text informing people living in Northern Nigerians to avoid the consumption of Palm oil that it has been poisoned. It took the intervention of Consumer Protection Agency to debase the text. There are several such text messages touching on all issues and it is a disturbing trend of unconventional form of citizen journalism.

Concerns

Banda (2010) notes that Journalism practice is often underpinned by a shared sense of values. This is translated into a set of ethos or ethics, represented in codes of ethical principles. These may be an appropriation of internationally agreed ethical standards and contextualised to guide the practices and routines in a given media institution.

Journalism ethos centre's on the principle of good practice as applicable to the specific challenges faced by journalists. It is widely known to journalists as their professional code of ethics which is usually statements drafted by both professional journalism associations and individual print, broadcast, and online news organizations to guide the professional conducts of journalists.

Niles (2007), notes that journalism code of ethics are principles that help separate the good writers and publishers from the frauds and con artists. The ethics of online journalism are ultimately, not different from the ethics of mainstream journalism. Singar (2010) notes that the online platform has present varying enthusiasm for users. It also involves some ethical issues that require reconsideration.

The Society of Professional Journalists has articulated a comprehensive policy of journalism ethics that can help guide any conscientious online writer. Besides the popular codes, such as objectivity, fairness, confidentiality of sources, protection of children and minors, Niles (2007), identified some widely accepted ethical factors that affect journalism and the ethical expectations (see Table 3).

These ethical elements are often not strictly adhered to in citizen journalism practice. There are ethical disregards in reports, videos, audio and pictures sent or posted by citizens. Leach (2009) in line with this development notes that what appears on Web sites and on blogs is not generally regarded as adhering to standards that govern news organizations. There exist areas of disconnect between the practices of journalists and the emerging conventions of digital/social media which demonstrate the need for ethical guidelines.

He identified some areas of ethical issues. These included: (1) Authenticating sources of information, especially when they are provided by an anonymous source, (2) assuring the reliability of information on linked sites, (3) dealing with conflicts of interest, and (4) concerns involving lack of oversight or accountability.

Citizen journalism is obviously a transformation in the practice of Journalism but it has also drawn some criticism as it relates to ethical conduct. Maher, (2005) points out that it has drawn criticism from traditional media like the New York Times, which have accused proponents of public journalism of abandoning the traditional goal of 'objectivity'. Many traditional journalists view citizen journalism with some scepticism, believing that only trained journalists can understand the exactitude and ethos involved in reporting news.

Table 3. Factors affecting journalism

Factor	Expectation
Differentiate	Differentiate between facts and opinions.
Accuracy	Check your facts before you publish.
Originality	Do not plagiarize and do link to all references.
Preservation	Don't make digital modifications that change the meaning or context of pictures or video footage
Authenticity	Don't submit "posed" pictures as true news.
Safety	Don't put yourself in danger in order to get that "great" story or picture.
Honesty	Be honest
Authenticating Sources	Make personal contact with the person(s) you are writing about and link to their online material (e.g. blog) if they have any.
Transparency	Be sure to disclose any personal relationship you may have to the story you publish

One of the challenges of citizen journalism is regulating its operation. Heald (2010) posits that regulation and professionalization of online journalism news sites and blogs have continued to pose a major challenge to journalism practice, That, lapses often emerge in areas such as building consumer awareness of websites, asking why many sites do not provide adequate information on what the site is, who funds it, what the sources are and who the author is. Another issue is how to authenticate online commenting. Some news organizations or journalists use pseudonyms to comment on and hence promoted their own articles. All these fall short of ethical standard.

A critical look at other areas of journalism ethos, such as authenticating sources, obviously shows that there are lapses. For example, on 30th May 2011, VOA Hausa service carried a report on the Mammy Market bomb blast in Bauchi State, Nigeria. The VOA correspondent reported and aired the voice of someone who claimed to be medical doctor and that he saw 10 corpses of the bomb blast victim which was an unconfirmed figure from an unknown source. The current security challenge (insurgence) in Nigeria is characterised by exaggerated figures of the numbers of deaths as a result of insurgents' attacks. Most times eyewitness reports exaggerate figures. For example, a recent attack on Gamboru Ngala by the insurgents on May 7 2014 the breaking news from various online sites reported that over 300 people were killed some eye witnesses reported that over 600 people, CNN reported that "at least 150 people dead…" Another example is the number of the abducted schoolgirls in Chibok, Nigeria by the insurgents, has still not been ascertained, which among other reason has compelled the Federal government to set up a committee to look into the abduction saga. The main worry is the inability of the citizen journalists to concede to others the right to publish or broadcast what they consider good enough.

Otufodunrin (2012) notes that there are too many unverified reports posted by people using various platforms. People send comments or reports on websites and don't want to be moderated even when the words used are unduly abusive, "Freedom without responsibility is very dangerous" Frommer (2009) commented on the issue of false citizen journalism practice. "CNN's iReport citizen journalism site was vandalized again with a false report claiming that AT&T CEO Randall Stephenson was 'found dead in his multimillion dollar beachfront mansion' after a coke binge with 'male dancers everywhere,'" he said. "[I]n 2010 an 18-year-old iReport prankster reported falsely that Apple CEO Steve Jobs had died of an apparent heart attack." Frommer (2009) commented further. "This highlights the risk of high-profile news organizations like CNN running citizen journalism sites," he said. "While CNN includes a disclaimer on all of its pages that stories have not been vetted or fact-checked, it's still going to offer an added air of credibility over a random, blank site," he continued. "And while it's good that CNN is able to take fraudulent posts like this one down so quickly, it's still going to be hard to ever achieve credibility when your platform is also being used for malice," he continued.

Gahran (2005) notes that all forms of journalism especially citizen journalism, face ethical quandaries. Three of the thorniest issues in journalism ethos are independence, objectivity, and transparency. Too many open Citizen Journalism (citJ) sites (especially those sponsored by news organizations) don't require or even facilitate transparency. That is, they generally don't require the people who post content to clarify how they are related to or involved in the story. These make it difficult for the audience to put citJ and other contributed content into perspective (Gahran, 2005). He adds that unfortunately the idea of transparency is all too frequently violated. Journalism fails to say anything about methods, motives, and sources. These are challenges on ethos for citizen journalism practice which also pose a great threat for a credible journalism practice.

Bugeja (2008) notes that increasingly with the advent of interactivity wireless and portable technologies, a reporter or freelancer must guard against issues in respect of posts on the internet because it is an ethical issue that touches on such matters as credibility, conflict of interest, fairness and discretion. Some of the challenges as it relates to ethos in respect of citizen journalism in Nigeria include; accuracy, challenge, transparency, authenticating sources, assuring the reliability of information, accountability/social responsibility, issues of opinion and fact.

Accuracy

Accuracy still counts in online or citizen journalism even if it's now known as content generation (In-Went capacity Buidling International, 2009).   It is common to see post on blog sites with report that is far from the truth or the truth tilted to suit the citizen journalist's purpose. Such reports usually not accompanied by links to substantiate such posts. For example Samson (2011), identifies some post on various networking sites during the violence that followed the presidential election in 2011 in Nigeria on Facebook, twitter, YouTube etc., many posted regular update on the crisis:

Shaheed Maikudi: "there is no killing of anybody in kaduna, there's serious protest, infact protesters are been executed by military men and men of the Nigerian Police. In fact even the burning of tyres has stoped. ....t".

Kels (@kelemukah), "Fitin in sme prts of northern Nigeria + d Wuse market area of Abuja as a result of d outcome of d presidential election.warn pple u knw"

These tweets were distortion of the fact as they did not reflect the true situation. Recently, most mainstream media organizations and several blog posted a news story accompanied by picture, that the American Marines that arrived Nigeria as part of US assistance to Nigeria to trace the abducted Chibok schoolgirls have made their first arrest of two suspected Boko Haram members in Benue State (North Central Nigeria). The headline read (US Marines carry out first arrests of two Boko Haram members in Benue State" The military spokesman of Nigeria refuted the report. As no American Marine had been deployed to any part of Nigeria as at when the media released the report.

Other widely tweeted and reported issues on the abducted school girls in Chibok Nigeria that were false or unauthenticated include: "Abducted Chibok Girls Seen In Central Africa"; "Breaking news: kidnapped girls raped 15 times daily — escaped girl confessed"; "Breaking News: Abducted Girls Reported seen around Gwoza"; "US Marin Loate Kidnaped School Girls in Sambisa Forest Using Surveillance Equipment."

It could be argued that citizen journalism is not the widely known conventional Journalism and thus the issue of ethos can be downplayed especially considering the difficulty in enforcing ethos or ethics on citizens. According to Hanson (2008) in journalism, informing people must come first and a responsible practitioner leans towards disseminating information but he or she has a responsibility not to kill a disturbing story or photo but to present it in a way that minimizes pain without holding back what the public needs to know. These channels used by Nigeria undoubtedly have policies that shield them from taking responsibility of inaccurate reports or manipulated videos and pictures but Hanson (2008) notes that there are cases when news organizations must withhold information. This is to guard against chaos in a peaceful society. Citizen Journalism might be an all comers affair but the managers of channels through which practitioners information are disseminated have a responsibility of serving as gate keepers to check the reports that negates journalistic ethical provisions or ethos.

Authenticating Sources

This is also a common ethical issue in Nigeria Citizen journalism practice. This trend is inherent with the text and calls made by citizen to international radio station. People also send tweets and post to other social networking sites without concrete identification of such sources.

Assuring the reliability of information, accountability/ social responsibility, issues of opinion and fact. Samson (2011) further identified some of such posts.

The following tweet by a mischievous fellow regarding Monday's post-election violence is one of such. Adam Sani (@abuabdallah92), who refused to put up a profile picture, tweeted:

"what we vote is not what we will be given, so we cant stay at home, we must come out and slaught every xtian in kaduna."

In less than 5 minutes, the tweet generated an outcry and was circulated round generating differing opinions with most condemning the malicious tweet:

Ify Diani (@Taki_Liverbird): "But this @abuabdallah92 dude is a big fool. He wants christians slaughtered. Blame hin and his ilk for these riots, not Buhari. #ThinkPeople"

Still on the ethical issue on authenticating sources and responsible journalism, on 25th February, 2011, Nairaland published a post that reads:

"Military Coup In Nigeria: This is my very first post on nairaland. I am still trying to figure things out but i would go straight to the point. A military coup is being plotted right now. I cannot disclose my real identity becos i fear for my safety. I was trying to create a blog site but i came across this website and i registered. There has been heavy military presence in places that we presume might give us problems. I pity Mr. jonathan."

There were several such posts by Nigerians that fall short of nearly all standards of journalism ethos. It is worrisome that this development observably is fostering division among Nigerians especially along ethnic and religious lines, as these sites and radio stations have wide followership, participation and their online posts/comments are believable by Nigerians.

Believability of Citizens Online Posts

It is obvious from the discussion above that there are ethical concerns in citizen journalism practice in Nigeria. However, what is of interest is that, it is observable that people, believe the ubiquitous information they see posted online even when sometimes things posted are not true or the truth distorted. It is also observable that people who read such online posts or text messages either start circulating it or send comments that seem to confirm their acceptance or believability without really verifying the truth from other available sources. The questions that readily come to mind are why do people believe these citizens online posts? How can people sift through the ubiquitous citizens' information and know what to trust?

Kiousis (2001) and Johnson and Kaye (2009) point out that when individual users rely more on a specific medium for information, they consider it to be more credible than other media; and that individual blog readers who rely on blogs for information are likely to consider blogs as more credible sources than other media (Kang, 2010). For example, Seipp (2002) points out that blog users relied considerably more on blog than other information sources for information and knowledge of and interest on issues which often becomes the strongest predication for visiting and believing such blogs.

The socio-cultural diversity of the Nigerian State plays a vital role in shaping or influencing array of issues such as governance, education, employment, media etc. It is observable that media credibility and believability is sometimes influenced by audience socio -cultural affiliation and trust in whether government or a political or regional affiliation. Tremayne (2007) examined the blog use for information in the context of the America/Iraq War and notes that trust in government positively predicted reliance on blog for war information despite relatively low political trust among blog users. Tremayne further notes that Conservative group of blog users trust the Conservative Bush Administration which translated into visiting blog sites supporting the war effort. These socio-cultural affiliations are identified by Names, religion, geopolitical origin etc. For example, a media organization owned by individual(s) from Northern Nigeria may enjoy higher credibility and believability rating among the Northerners than a media organization owned by individual(s) from the Southern part of Nigeria and vice-versa. Looking at citizen online posts in Nigeria, it is observable that the believability and credibility is high when an individual who has the same religious affiliation and geopolitical origin with the audience posts it. In this case sifting of citizen online post and believability is often determined by religious and geopolitical affiliation. Similarly, Taylor (2006) notes that, individual's judge credibility based on level of believability and community affiliation. Believability is a subjective measure of fairness, accuracy and bias which matters to audience of media platform that stays involved in their communities to build local relationship and close association with audience. The closer a citizen journalism source is to the community the more believable (Taylor, 2006).

A stereotype held by Nigerians about the traditional media (radio, television and newspapers) is another reason why Nigerians believe online citizen posts. It is observable that Nigerians hold stereotype about the traditional media as a result of media ownership and prolonged military leadership. Nigerians are of the opinion that Media owners influence media reports and that media pursue subjective consideration against the pursuit of truth and so have become compartmentalized to suit group of interests which in most cases are the proprietor's interests. These have compelled Nigerians to crave for other sources of information and the online posts have come handy. Kenya serves as an excellent example following the contested elections there in December 2007, around 600 blogs appeared in the web, many debating issues concealed by the established Kenyan media.

Nigerians often believe citizen posts because sometimes they uncover issues concealed by mainstream Nigerian media.

Until recently when the Nigerian state underwent a measure of stability, with the advent of democracy, the socio-political environment had been marked by periodical political and social instability which kept military in power for a long time. The military dictatorship created a scenario of secrecy and high handedness on the media. These affected media performance, which Nnamani (2003) points out that hitherto one easy claim of the Nigerian press is that even though the country is in a democracy, it appears slightly difficult to pick valid information since according to them, much of the system still carries the exclusivity and secrecy of the past military order. Nnamani (2003) further notes that *"speculative journalism took centre stage. 'Rumour' or 'concoction' became substitutes for information flow and the governed became easy preys of such concocted news items"*.

Credibility ratings or ranking of media organizations among Nigerians is another factor responsible for believing online posts. For example, in Erdos and Morgan (2008) survey on American opinion leaders ranked BBC News one of the most objective and credible U.S. news sources (BBC, 2008). There exist such credibility rankings among media audience in Nigeria. For example, it is observable that an average Northern Nigerian listener of the Hausa Services of the British Broadcasting Corporation ranks BBC Hausa Service high in terms of credibility content. It is common to hear a Nigerian refer to BBC news, Aljazeera, Sahara Reporters, and Premium News etc. as their sources of latest information. Hence whatever report is posted and accessed online via these media have high believability standing among Nigerians except proven otherwise by other media with the same credibility ranking.

Opinion leaders also play a role in the believability of online posts. Opinion leaders could range from religious leaders, heads of peer and social groups, head of family etc. This factor reflects the 1940 study of social influence that states that media effect are indirectly established through the personal influence of opinion leaders. Majority of people receive much of their information and are influenced by the media second hand through the personal influence of opinion leader. These opinion leaders gain their influence through more elite media such as online posts, news websites as opposed to mainstream media. In this process social influence is created and they then begin to disseminate these opinions through the public who become opinion followers (Baran, 2002). Nigerians have several social for a where individual exercise certain influence either as a result the person's social standing or appointment. These opinion leaders disseminate information from online post and followers believe these posts with little or no confirmation from other sources. For example, a religious cleric reads an online post and tells followers about it who in turn believe and spread same information.

Another reason Nigerians believe online posts is the opportunity of accessing several similar or related online posts on several news websites which serves as a sort of verification. This reason also serves as an avenue for sifting, which post is true and which one is not. The verification opportunity made available through related links increases the level of believability of online posts and sifting true from false post. For example, if a citizen sends a posts on twitter or Facebook, Nigerians take another step of connecting to other sites to verify the stories or send text messages friends or relation who lives in an area an incidence occurred. For example, all National newspapers in Nigeria are online, hence, citizen verify reports from the sites of these dailies and other sites. Another example is the news of the plane crash of 2 June 2012 in Nigeria that claimed the lives of over 150 passengers started as a rumour but within 2 hours, several citizens had posted about the events in various online channels and online media organization had given a breaking news. The posts on several websites as a sort of verification make online posts believable.

Conclusion

Citizen Journalism obviously has given individual opportunity to disseminate information and essentially, it has profound implications for the flourishing of society in areas such as democracy (Salawu, 2011). Banda (2010) adds that the overall importance of citizen journalism would seem to lie in its ability to engender some action on the part of authorities and other interested groups in response to perceived citizens' felt needs. Change is imperative as Zachary, (2006) notes that it is already clear that a new journalism ethos is required; a new way of thinking and acting that acknowledges the criticisms and doubt that citizen journalists/ authors may never adopt journalistic standard from the parties involved.

Although a new way of thinking and acting that acknowledges the criticisms and doubt that citizen journalists/ authors may never adopt journalistic standard from the parties involved (Zachary, 2006), it is still imperative to consider the issue of ethos in this open source journalism, and how to regulate activities of the great number of participants, just to ensure the health of the society. No doubt, Citizen Journalism has brought forth an unprecedented flowering of news and information to an array of audience. But, it has also destabilized the old business models that have supported quality journalism for decades.

The growing concern in respect to non-adherence consideration of journalistic ethos in citizen journalism in Nigeria is observably propelled by the medium or channels citizens' use. The international broadcast organizations like the BBC Hausa service, VOA Hausa Service, Radio France International Deutch Wella Radio that have wide listenership especially in Northern Nigeria give listeners the opportunity to make phone calls and send text messages to live news programmes. These contributions from the audience are usually characterized by issues, which fall short of journalism ethos.

Social networks such as Facebook and twitter are some of the widely used platforms by Nigerians for posting matters bothering on nearly everything (health, music, governance, politics, economy, etc. and in some cases provide links to some news stories. The phone-to-phone form of citizen journalism, although it is an informal kind of citizen journalism but it is one of the effective form of citizen journalism that is totally devoid of any elements of ethos. People receive and spread text and multimedia messages which often have no authenticated source. Citizen may seem not to be organized like the conventional journalism but efforts can be made to inject some sanity to citizen's posts. For examplem Lewenstein (2008) points out that subscribers to online service such as the ComNet which offers a wide range of interactivity services agreed to abide by services rules of behaviour which include prohibitions against objectionable or lewd language, and use only their true names.

Regulating activities of citizen journalists is an important step in addressing the challenges in respect of disregard for journalistic ethos, especially the citizen journalism version promoted by international media which has in recent times fuelled unpleasant situation such ass inciting Nigerians. It might be difficult to regulate phone to phone (text) information dissemination but other forms can be checked or facilitated by agencies like the Nigeria Broadcasting Commission and Nigeria Union of Journalists should work towards regulating other forms of practice. For example, British National Union of Journalists (BNUJ) has published its new "code of practice" for what it calls "witness contributors".

Regulation can start somewhere, particularly with those who play the role of gatekeeper in media organizations and other channels. For example, Kiss (2011) notes that in respect BNUJ, that the code is intended "for publishers of citizen journalism designed to encourage responsible and ethical use of user-generated material". The online media or host sites could also adopt strict measures on the kind of information citizen upload on websites. Creating awareness on issues of ethos is important so that citizens can imbibe ethos that makes for meaningful participation.

Blogs and online posts are and would remain sources of information to the global internet public (In-Went Capacity Building International, 2009). Worldwide blogging and other forms of citizen journalism have increased in Nigeria in recent years. Observably, Nigerians believe and will continue to believe these online posts. Thus as audience continue to sift online posts to authenticate reports, it is worthy of note that Journalistic ethos cannot be neglected because of the assumption that citizen journalists would not adhere. Ethos is still valid in the era of digital media.

References

Banda, F. (2010) Citizen journalism &democracy in Africa: An exploratory study; South Africa, Highway Africa

Baran, S. (2002) Theories of Mass Communication Introduction to Mass Communication McGraw-Hill.

Bryan S. Turner (2006) "Communitarianism." The Cambridge Dictionary of Sociology. Cambridge: Cambridge University Press.

Bugeja, M. (2008) "To post or not to post: the question for writers in the digital age" Media Ethics: Issues and Cases 6th Ed. New York: McGraw-Hil Coy

Flew, T. (2008) New media: An introduction. Melbourne, Oxford University Press

Gillmore, D. (2006) We the media: grassroots journalism by the people, for the people. Cambridge, O'Reilly.

Glaser, M. (2004, 17 November). The new voices: Hyperlocal citizen media sites want you. Online Journalism Review.

Hanson, C. (2008) "Informing the Public Must Come First" `in: Media Ethics: Issues and Cases (6th ed.). New York, McGraw-Hill Coy.

Johnson, T. J. & Kaye, B. K. (2009). In blog we trust? Deciphering credibility of components of the internet among politically interested internet users. Computers in Human Behavior, 25, 175-182.

Kang, M. (2010). Measuring social media credibility: A study on a measure of blog credibility. Submitted to the Institute for Public Relations for the 2009 Ketchum Excellence in Public Relations Research Award.

Kiousis, S. (2001) Public trust or mistrust? Perceptions of media credibility in the information age. Mass Communication and Society, 4(4), 381-403.

Maher, V. (2005) Citizen journalism is dead. New media lab, School of Journalism & Media Studies, Rhodes University, South Africa.

McQuail, D. (2000) McQaiul's Communication Theory, (4th ed) , London, Sage Publication.

Olubunmi P. A., Caroline H.,Debra, B, Richard L. (2011) How technology transforms journalism business through citizen-reporters in Nigeria. International Journal of Strategic Information Technology and Applications. 2(2), 1-11

Patterson, P. (2008) An introduction to ethical decisions making. Media Ethics: Issues and cases (6th ed.). New York: McGraw-Hil Coy

Salawu, A. (2011) Citizen Journalism Off-Line: The (Nigerian) Punch Model, Estudos em Comunicao No. 9. 185-196

Seipp, C. (2002) Online uprising. American Journalism Review. 24(13), 42-47

Singer, B.J. (2010) Norms and the network: Journalism ethics in a shared media space. In Meyers C. (ed) Journalism ethics: A philosophical approach. Oxford: Oxford University Press.

Taylor, H.S. (2006) The executive blog as a communications tool. Califonia, ProQuest

Tremayne, M. (2007) Blogging, Citizenship, and the Future of Media. London: Routledge

Wilson, J. (2012) Ethical issues in citizen journalism practice in Nigeria. In Wilson D. (ed.) Media, Terrorism, political communication and multicultural environment, Nigeria, African Council for Communication Education (pages 123-140)

Documentation

BBC Press Office (2008, 11 November) BBC news U.S. ranking. Retrieved 4/6/2012 from www.bbc.co.uk/pressoffice/bbcworldeide/worldwidestoriies/pressreleases/2008/11_november/bbc_news_us_ranking.shtml

Bowman, S. and Willis, C. (2003) We media: How audiences are shaping the future of news and information. The Media Center, American Press Institute. http://www.hypergene.net/wemedia/weblog.php

Frommer, D. (2009, 27 July), CNN's iReport vandalized again with false report claiming CEO's death, coke binge. Business Insider SAI, Retrieved 12/9/2013 from http://www.businessinsider.com/cnns-ireport-vandalized-again-with-false-report-claiming-ceos-death-2009-7

Dvorkin, J.A. (2005, 27 January) Media matters: Can public radio journalism be re-invented? National Public Radio, http://www.npr.org/yourturn/ombudsman/010705.html

Edmonds, R (2011) As blogs and citizen journalism grow, where's the news? Poynter, http://www.poynter.org/uncategorized/71962/as-blogs-and-citizen-journalism-grow-wheres-the-news/

Gahran , A. (2006, 26 January) UK: New code of practice for witness contributors IReport. Retrieved http://www.ireporter.org/ethics/

Gahran, A. (2005, 27 June). Objectivity, independence, and transparency: Three-legged stool? IReport, Retrieved 12/6/2014 http://www.ireporter.org/2005/06/objectivity_ind.html#more

Gahran, A. (2005 4 November) Open CitJ Sites: Why not require transparency? IReport, http://www.ireporter.org/ethics/

Gaulin, P. (2007, 27 April) Are ethics missing in citizen journalism? Yahoo Contributor Network, http://contributor.yahoo.com/user/14067/pam_gaulin.html

Gillmor D. (2008, 14 July) Where did citizen journalist come from? Retrieved 12/6/2013 from http://citmedia.org/blog/2008/07/14/where-did-citizen-journalist-come-from/

Glaser, M. (2006, September 27). Your Guide to Citizen Journalism. Public Broadcasting Service. Retrieved 12/10/2011 from http://www.pbs.org/mediashift/2006/09/your-guide-to-citizen-journalism270.html

Guthrie L.S. (1994) Immanuel Kent and the Categorical Imperative, The Examined Life On-line Philosophy Journal. 2 (7) Retrieved from http://sguthrie.net/kant.htm

Heald, E (2010) The ethical and professional challenges in participative online media in the Arab world, newsrooms and journalism. Retrieved 12/6/2013 from http://www.editorsweblog.org/newsrooms_and_journalism/2010/06/the _ethical_and_professional_challenges.php

Idowu, L. (2012) Occupynigeria Protesters Take On News Media Coverage (Comment). Retrieved 9/2/2013 from http://www.cpj.org/blog/2012/01/occupynigeria-protesters-take-on-news-media-covera.php#comment-129441

In-Went capacity Buidling International (2009), Online journalism: opportunities and challenges for press freedom, IIJ Alumni Review, January 2009 - 2.02-0001-2009, Retrieved from www.inwent.org/iij

Keita, M. (2012) Occupy Nigeria protesters take on news media coverage. Retrieved 12/02/2012 from http://www.cpj.org/blog/2012/01/occupynigeria-protesters-take-on-news-media-covera.php (Accessed)

Kperogi F. (2011) Webs of Resistance: The Citizen Online Journalism of the Nigerian Digital Diaspora, the Department of Communication at Digital Archive @ GSU Retrieved 12/10/2012 from http://digitalarchive.gsu.edu/cgi/viewcontent.cgi?article=1027&context=communication_diss

Lasica, J.D. (2003) "What is Participatory Journalism?", Online Journalism Review, August 7, Retrieved from http://www.ojr.org/ojr/workplace/1060217106.php

Leach, J. (2009) Creating ethical bridges from journalism to digital news, Nieman Report. Retrieved 23/7/2013 from http://www.nieman.harvard.edu/reports/article/101899/Creating-Ethical-Bridges-From-Journalism-to--Digital-News.aspx

Meyer, P. (1995) paper presented at IRE conference on computer assisted reporting in Cleveland in September 1995. Retrieved 12/10/2011 from http://www.unc.edu/~pmeyer/ire95pj.htm

Merritt, D. (2004, September 29) News media must regain vigor, courage., PJNet Today. Retrieved from http://pjnet.org/post/318/

Meyer, E.P. (1995). Public journalism and the problem of objectivity. Retrieved 12/10/2011 from http://www.unc.edu/~pmeyer/ire95pj.htm

Murdarasi, K. (2008) Aristotle's golden mean ethics: classic moral theory from the Nichomachean ethics. Retrieved 12/10/2011from http://karenmurdarasi.suite101.com/aristotle-golden-mean

Niles, R. (2007) What are the ethics of online journalism? ORJ Online Journalism Review . Retrieved from http://www.ojr.org/ojr/wiki/ethics/

Oak, M. (2011) Positive effect of the Media. Retrieved 25/5/2012 from www.buzzle.com/articles/positive-effect-of-the-media.html

Nnamani, C (2003) The Press and the Nigerian Project, A public lecture of the Newspaper Proprietors Association of Nigeria (NPAN) Diamond Hall, Golden Gate Restaurant, Ikoyi, Lagos. Thursday, 23rd October 2003.

Olakitan, Y. (2012) How New Media is affecting Traditional Journalism in Nigeria, Retrieved 12/02/2012   from http://www.twitterjournalism.com/tag/marriage/

Otufodunrin L. (2012) Occupynigeria-Protesters-Take-on-news-media-cover: comments. Retrieved 12/10/2011 from http://www.cpj.org/blog/2012/01/occupynigeria-protesters-take-on-news-media-covera.php#comment-129202

Rogers, T. (2011) Journalism and the Egyptian Uprising, About.com Journalism. Retrieved 12/10/2011from http://journalism.about.com/od/citizenjournalism/a/whatiscitizen.htm

Samson, K. (22nd April, 2011) The New Media and The Nigerian Citizen Journalist. Naijastories.com, Retrieved 12/10/2011from http://www.naijastories.com/2011/04/the-new-media-and-the-nigerian-citizen-journalist/

Zachary P. G. (2006) Truth or Consequences: The Future of the Journalist in America, Retrieved 12/02/2012 from http://www.dvorak.org/blog/essays/zachary1.htm

Section 2: Identity and Culture

The Guy Fawkes Mask as Visual Communication of the Internet Group Anonymous.

Lars Konzack

Abstract: The Guy Fawkes mask has become a symbol of the internet group Anonymous. This paper seeks to understand why this happened. The Guy Fawkes Mask takes us back to a 17th Century Catholic renegade, a 1980s graphic novel, a millennial movie based on the graphic novel, social media visual communication practicing internet memes on 4chan and YouTube, and physical demonstrations in public space. It will show how the Guy Fawkes Mask changed meaning during this process, and how this symbol works as a meaningful signifier in a digital age.

Keywords: Anonymous, Guy Fawkes Mask, Internet trolling

The Mask

To fully understand this phenomenon it is important to explain how a mask works. The anthropologist Roger Caillois explains the function of play has on society. He recognizes the mask as "a sacred object universally present, whose transformation into a plaything perhaps marks a prime mutation in the history of civilization" (Caillois 2001, p.59). And later he asserts: "On occasion of unrestrained excitement or riot, which is popular and valued for its excess, the use of masks is supposed to reinvigorate, renew, and recharge both nature and society" (Caillois 2001, p.87). This tells us that the mask plays a central role to civilization; it has deconstructive and subversive effects to society and is recognized as a device for rebellious behavior. But the mask is more than that; it works as an identity marker as well. Normally one would say that the true identity is behind the mask. An identity may be masked in a way that nobody will be able to find the true identity of the masked person. However, the mask can become an identity in its own right when used as a shared identity (Jacquet-Chiffelle et al. 2009, p.82):

"Virtual persons play the role of a mask. In front of the mask we have the identity. Several physical persons can hide behind the mask. When several persons share an identity, they are all linked to the same virtual person. The shared identity becomes in our model a shared virtual identity."

The idea of the shared identity is crucial in order to understand the internet group Anonymous' use of the mask. The wearer is no longer an individual but has symbolically become a part of the Anonymous collective. This is needed because *"Anonymous is not a singular organization or even a single network, rather it is a series of networks and networked actors that share a complex of memes. Individual operations reflect the interests of unique actors or activist networks"* (Jarvis 2014: 331). In order to make Anonymous function outside the context of the Internet there had to be a shared symbol of unity as well as a shared symbol of anonymity.

A Short History of the Guy Fawkes Mask

Guy Fawkes (1570-1606) was a member of a group of provincial English Catholics who planned the failed Gunpowder Plot with the aim to blow up the English parliament in 1605. Guy Fawkes was sentenced to death. The night of the plot was November 5th and has become a British national holiday – the so-called Guy Fawkes Night in which the British people arrange bonfires and set off fireworks, burning a Guy Fawkes figure and by doing so celebrating the capture of this terrorist.

The symbolic position of Guy Fawkes changed when creative writer Alan Moore during the 1980s wrote a masterpiece of a graphic novel titled V for

Vendetta. Set in a near-future dystopian fascist England, the main character, a vigilante, dress up as Guy Fawkes like a super-hero or to be more precise a super-anti-hero. Though he has no other superpowers than deception and drug-fuelled ingenuity, this mysterious character named V, plans to bring down the fascist government.

Later in 2005, the V for Vendetta graphic novel was turned into a movie. This vulgar version of Moore's vision, however, was unsatisfactory to Alan Moore and he demanded not to be credited for this work (Lamont 2011). Nonetheless, the character V became more well-known to the public and in 2006 spawned a short-lived internet meme known as Epic Fail Guy (see Figure 1).

Figure 1. Epic Fail Guy.

Epic Fail Guy features a dancing stickman wearing a Guy Fawkes mask, making fun of geeks trying too hard to be cool. The ironic and self-ironic Internet meme Epic Fail Guy originated from the image- and messageboard 4chan (Pittaway 2012, Nail 2013), and 4chan also happens to be the birthplace for the Internet group Anonymous (Stryker 2011, Olson 2012). The link to Guy Fawkes and V for Vendetta is well-known but Epic Fail Guy has been overlooked by many researchers (Call 2008, Kohns 2013, Jarvis 2014).

During this process the Guy Fawkes symbol has changed its meaning. For several hundreds of years he was the symbol of avoiding and disabling a vindictive malevolent act against the English parliament, burning the evils against society away. It wasn't until Alan Moore's vision of a vigilante anti-hero fighting a fascist regime, the idea of a Guy Fawkes mask hatched. In his view Guy Fawkes became a symbol of a righteous fight against oppression. This symbolic meaning of Guy Fawkes was continued in the movie. Nevertheless, the Epic Fail Guy internet meme changed the meaning of this symbol one more time. The Epic Fail Guy symbolizes gawky guys trying to be cool and failing in that attempt and failed endeavors in general.

Protesters

In February 2008, the internet group Anonymous decided to target The Church of Scientology in two ways: 1) they blocked Scientology websites with coordinated DDoS-attacks, and 2) for the first time manifested public demonstrations while wearing masks, because they didn't wanted to be recognized by Scientology since the organization had been known to target critics of the Church of Scientology personally, singling out individuals and making false accusations against them in old media such as newspapers, radio and television (Kohns 2013).

In late January 2008, a two-minute YouTube video "Message to Scientology" had gone viral within the Anonymous collective, telling everyone the reasons why they did not like Scientology and how they aimed at dismantling the organization (churfofscientology 2008). The mood and tone was sinister and ended by saying:

116

We are Anonymous. We are legion. We never forgive. We never forget. Expect us!

Even though there was no Guy Fawkes mask presented in the YouTube video, the demonstrators ended up wearing masks or in other ways disguising their face. Different masks were being used, but the most commonly used mask happened to be the Guy Fawkes mask from the fairly recent V for Vendetta movie. The message was an in-joke referring to the Epic Fail Guy meme, insinuating that indeed Scientology was an epic fail. But it was a complex symbolism, because it also stated:

we may be the epic fail guys of the Internet, but we are still stronger than Scientology.

And at the same time it shouted out that Anonymous is vigilante internet group just like in V for Vendetta, fighting for justice in a grim world of injustice. What had just been an in-joke at first grew to be the symbol of Anonymous in the following years; especially by the Occupy Movement from 2011, not forgetting the Arab Spring of the same year (Paget 2012). The Arab Spring was widely supported by the internet Anonymous that helped by attacking the oppressive North-African government's digital infrastructure and by circulating information about the rebellion to the Western old media news distribution.

Oliver Kohn writes: "From a purely functional perspective, it may suffice to leave it at that observation: The Guy Fawkes mask symbolizes, as it were, the unity of protest and thus makes the protest recognizable as such. The 'iconography of revolt' therefore plays as much a part in the 'reportage-stylevisual journalism' as it does in staging this revolt. On both levels, the Guy Fawkes mask functions as a symbol of the protest movement's unity." (Kohn 2013: 93).

The importance of the Guy Fawkes mask as a symbol became obvious when Shepard Fairey, the man behind Barack Obama's Hope propaganda poster of 2008, envisioned the Occupy Movement. Fairey chose to depict a protester wearing a Guy Fawkes mask as the symbol of rebellion in the 21st Century. But this artistic occurrence also showed that the protesters didn't accept any interpretation of the Occupy movement. At first Shepard Fairey wrote on the Occupy-poster: *Mister President, we HOPE you're on our side.* This was later changed to: *We are the HOPE.* This significant alteration was due to the fact that the Occupy movement was non-partisan (Gray 2011).

Confronted with the way the internet group Anonymous had suddenly used the Guy Fawkes mask, Alan Moore expressed his thoughts and feelings on the matter (Lamont 2011):

"It turns protests into performances. The mask is very operatic; it creates a sense of romance and drama. I mean, protesting, protest marches, they can be very demanding, very gruelling. They can be quite dismal. They're things that have to be done, but that doesn't necessarily mean that they're tremendously enjoyable – whereas actually, they should be"

While Alan Moore was dissatisfied with the 2005 Hollywood movie visualization of his graphic novel, he was apparently overjoyed by this turn of events, when he later wrote: "It also seems that our character's charismatic grin has provided a ready-made identity for these highly motivated protesters, one embodying resonances of anarchy, romance, and theatre that are clearly well-suited to contemporary activism, from Madrid's Indignados to the Occupy Wall Street movement" (Moore 2012).

YouTube warning and protest videos

In 2006 Time Magazine chose the Person of the Year as YOU, because the Internet was giving the freedom to each and every one to express themselves through user-generated content on websites like blogs,

MySpace and YouTube. Five years later, in the wake of the Arab Spring and the Occupy movement, Time Magazine chose The Protester as Person of the Year. The link between these two events was that now people of the Internet were using their power of participation and collaboration to express their frustration and dissatisfaction with the current political affairs whether it was the bankers of Wall Street or despots of North Africa. Everyone could make their own YouTube videos – not just the media industry. Jay Rosen recognized this shift when saying: "The people formerly known as the audience wish to inform the media people of our existence, and a shift in power that goes with the platform shift you've all heard about" (Rosen 2012, p. 13).

Countless of Anonymous YouTube videos have been made. They are usually short between two to five minutes long – like a music video. Most of them follow more or less the same schema. First there is an intro with grandiose music, then follows clips of masked protesters and/or other thought-provoking images and a male monotonous and anonymized voice telling the message of an upcoming operation or other news. The video normally ends with the motto or a variation of the motto:

We are Anonymous. We are legion. We never forgive. We never forget. Expect us!

Another approach is a simple YouTube video with a young man in black clothes wearing a a Guy Fawkes mask, making gestures while a monotonous and anonymized voice tells the message. It ends as always with the Anonymous motto.

Having said that these YouTube videos follow a schema does not mean there aren't any variations. Sometimes there is a female voice instead. Sometimes the message is written in the video while the monotonous voice reads the message aloud. And sometimes a lot of effort is put into the video and it turns into a surprisingly new experience not like any other of the videos. Still the ending with the motto remains, and the carried message is the important meaning of the video.

Usually, but not always, the message of the video is written down below YouTube video in the text-box, so the viewer does not have to watch and hear the video if s/he just want to read the message without the images. Often the message in the YouTube video is a warning that some organization or government is going to be attacked by the Anonymous collective.

Anonymous approved this message

The advantages of such a strategy of making YouTube videos based on a schema is that everyone, even if they have got no experience with making video at all, can make something that works and at least get the message out. The problem is that when everyone can claim to be Anonymous, it becomes unclear if the message is actually coming from Anonymous.

In the summer of 2011, a YouTube video titled "[VOSTFR] Message from Anonymous : Operation Facebook, Nov 5 2011" a warning of an upcoming DDoS attack against Facebook was delivered (LaughingOutLol 2001). The monotonous voice told that on November 5th (Guy Fawkes Day) Facebook would be destroyed. The confusion arose when Russia Today a couple of days later asked whether it was a hack or a hoax (TheAlyonaShow 2011). It was difficult to get a clear answer if this was an official Anonymous operation or a prank from someone just calling themselves Anonymous.

In the end Facebook wasn't attacked. It showed, nonetheless, that the non-leader organization had a structural weakness. When everybody could call themselves Anonymous, how could anybody know when it was the real Anonymous, or if there was a real Anonymous at all? When everyone wears a mask, it is impossible to truly distinguish friend from enemy. It becomes a masquerade in which nobody knows who is who.

120

Even so, the symbolic meaning of the Guy Fawkes mask could also be used by others who sympathized with their cause. In January 2012, members of the Polish parliament put on Guy Fawkes masks in protest against the The Anti-Counterfeiting Trade Agreement (ACTA) (Warman 2012, Jarvis 2014). It was a strong political signal against the treaty that was accused by Anonymous for suppressing Internet freedom. Later the same year, against all odds, ACTA was rejected by the EU parliament (Solon 2012). During the spring of 2012 protesters wearing the Guy Fawkes mask had opposed ACTA in the streets all over Europe, and the protesters had won the conflict.

The Guy Fawkes mask became a symbol of protests, or as Roger Caillois said, unrestrained riot and used to reinvigorate and renew society. Out of an old story about a plot against the British parliament came a new story in a graphic novel about an anti-hero bringing down fascism. And from this heritage it grew into an Internet meme and became the symbol of Internet vigilantism and rebellion against old media and old regimes, injustice and oppression. The Guy Fawkes mask turned protesters into a shared identity of fighting for a righteous cause of freedom on the Internet.

Origins of Geek Culture

But why would Anonymous choose a symbol taken from a movie or graphic novel when there are so many other symbols of protest they could choose from such as anarchist symbols, a raised fist, or even the image of Che Guevara? To understand this, we have to get a better understanding of where anonymous is coming from.

The group Anonymous originated from 4chan and as such they have a fairly short history, going back to when 4chan was launched in 2003. But as E. Gabriela Coleman has shown, the trolls of 4chan are linked back to earlier hacker culture and even the telephone phreaks of the 1960s (Coleman 2012). Actually, the term hacker originally meant someone who was very good at programming a computer, creating genius programs – and some of the first computer games like Space War from 1961 (Graetz 1981). Science fiction and computer games were to become a central part of what would later be known as geek culture. But what is geek culture and how is it different from popular culture?

First of all geek culture is not necessarily popular. Some cultural products are, some are not. In that respect it is not necessarily easy to distinguish geek culture from popular culture. However, it becomes very easy if you look at the fantasy it promotes. Geek culture offers escape into fantastic worlds that create spectacular visions of new realities, while popular culture offers an escape into a world much like our own. In fact, the audience of popular culture does not want to be challenged with something that could destroy the illusion that this is not real, and consequently visions of a long gone past or a far future come in the way of deserting into a false reality (Lewis 1969). Geek culture is on the other hand quite aware that this is not the real world and actually uses the fantasies to build and create new ideas. As J. R. R Tolkien wrote in his essay On Fairy-Stories (Tolkien 1997, p.144).

> *"Fantasy is a natural human activity. It certainly does not destroy or even insult Reason; and it does not either blunt the appetite for, nor obscure the perception of, scientific verity. On the contrary. The keener and the clearer is the reason, the better fantasy will it make."*

This question leads us back to no other than H. P. Lovecraft (1890-1937), an author from the beginning of the twentieth century who wrote horror stories and created his own mythology with grotesque monsters that ruled the universe. But he did more than that. He got in contact with the Amateur Press Association also known simply as APA, a way of distributing content outside formal channels within a group of people (Spencer, 1957). This gave H. P. Lovecraft the chance to produce and more importantly distribute literary criticism about horror stories, weird fiction, and science fiction. Among his most notable works is his essay "Supernatural Horror in Literature" (1927) that still to this day is considered a most important study about the horror literature as a genre (Kneale, 2006).

The works of Lovecraft and the circle of authors around him weren't appreciated by the established academia at the time so they had to invent their own channels for communication. The science fiction genre had the same problem and some of the people in the Lovecraft circle were science fiction writers as well. In 1930 science fiction enthusiasts came out with the first science fiction fanzine in which they could share literature, ideas and not least literary criticism of science fiction. Since the humanities of the established academia didn't take their literature seriously they had to invent their own alternative intellectual milieu, and in 1937, the very same year that H. P. Lovecraft died, the first science fiction APA called Fantasy Amateur Press Association (FAPA) was formed. This idea spread to other cultures outside what was accepted by established academia. Comics got their first APA called CAPA-alpha in 1964, and in 1975 Alarums and Excursions a role-playing game APA was introduced (Spencer, 1957; Sanders, 1994; Schelly, 2002; Peterson 2012). Lovecraftian horror stories, science fiction, comics, and role-playing games all had in common that they were outside the interests of the humanities of established academia and consequently had to invent their own alternative intellectual milieu that came to be known as fandom and geek culture. By doing this they were setting their own standards for cultural criticism outside academia.

What has all of this to do with Anonymous? Well, the heavy engine behind geek culture was science fiction fandom and this culture was well-established within American engineers and programmers. Actually one might argue that in fact geek culture originated from the culture of engineers and programmers. Science fiction fandom developed strong ties to geek culture such as comics and role-playing games. And the engineers and programmers not only read fantasy, science fiction, horror stories, comics about superhero vigilantes, and played role-playing games, they also invented the Internet back in the 1960s and 1970s (Berger, 1977; Rosenweig, 1998; Raymond, 2000; Feinemann, 2005; Coppa, 2006).

The Internet turned out to be the perfect platform for providing and communicating geek culture. Each and every fandom could make their bulletin board or forum on the Internet. Accordingly, geek culture grew at the same rate as the Internet grew, which meant that back in 1990s when the Internet became main-stream then geek culture became main-stream as well. This development hasn't stopped yet, and if this correlation continues, geek culture will be on its way to go from main-stream culture to become the dominating culture of the 21st Century.

So when 4chan was established as a platform for exchange of pictures and texts, it was only natural that they would use imagery and ideas from geek culture, because this was the culture of engineers and programmers, this was their cultural historical transition from demoted sub-culture to ruling culture. The character V from Vendetta worked as a symbol of this transition, breaking down the old world and creating a new one based on geek values and geek principles. Furthermore, Alan Moore was and is still one of the most recognized graphic novelists within comic book fandom (Brown, 1997; Parkin, 2011).

In that respect the mask is much more than a symbol of Anonymous, it becomes the symbol of a cultural change in which geek culture overshadow the old paradigms. It has become a symbol of fantasy and computer culture rather than old school of broadcasting and social realism of the twentieth century.

The Internet memes bring about an extra-academic cultural tradition that is about to leave the science fiction, fantasy and superhero ghetto behind, searching for new territories to conquer. They use Harry Potter, Dr. Who, Lord of the Rings, Call of Cthulhu, Game of Thrones, Batman, Spiderman, The Matrix, and Star Wars as their symbols. Not only that, they create their own symbols as a prolongation of this geek culture with memes such as Troll Face, Advice Dog, Socially Awkward Penguin, Disaster Girl, and Epic Fail Guy (Stryker, 2011; Shifman, 2014).

So in order to understand the Anonymous movement it is not enough just to comprehend the history of the Anonymous mask as a symbol, it is not enough to comprehend the actions of Anonymous, to fully understand Anonymous it is important to stress the ties to a growing geek culture that can be traced back to H. P. Lovecraft and the willingness to appreciate fantastic genres that the established academia left behind, and which is now becoming a cultural hegemonic force.

Conclusion

The Guy Fawkes mask has become the symbol of the vigilante group Anonymous. It originated from the 17th Century Catholic renegade Guy Fawkes who inspired Alan Moore's graphic novel V for Vendetta, later used in the movie V for Vendetta, which again inspired the self-ironic Internet meme Epic Fail Guy. It is a symbol of shared identity, anonymity and revolt. It has come to be used as a general symbol of Internet activism and protests against government and/or corporate oppression of Internet freedom. The symbol finds its roots within comic book fandom and in that respect it symbolizes the emerging hegemony of geek culture.

References

Berger, A. I. (1977, November). Science Fiction Fans in Socio-Economic Perspective. Factors in the Social Consciousness of a Genre. In: Science Fiction Studies, Vol. 4., No. 3, Nov. 1977, p. 232-46.

Brown, J. A. (1997). "Comic book fandom and cultural capital". *The Journal of Popular Culture 30.4 (1997)*, p. 13-31.

Caillois, R. (2001). *Man Play and Games*. Chicago: Illinois University press.

Call, L. (2008). "A is for Anarchy, V is for Vendetta: Images of Guy Fawkes and the Creation of Postmodern Anarchism". In: *Anarchist Studies, Volume 16, Issue 2, January 1, 2008*, p. 154-72.

Coppa, F. (2006).. "A Brief History of Media Fandom". In: Hellekson & Busse (ed.) *Fan fiction and fan communities in the age of the Internet: new essays*. Jefferson: McFarland, 2006, p. 41-59.

Coleman, E. G. (2012). "Phreaks, hackers, and Trolls: The Politics of Transgression and Spectacle". In: Mandiberg (ed.) *The Social Media Reader*. New York, NY: New York University Press.

Feinemann, N. (2005). *GeekChic: The Ultimate Guide to Geek Culture*. Corte Madera, CA: Gingko Press.

Graetz, J. M. (1981, August). "The origin of Spacewar". In: *Creative Computing 18 (1981)*. NJ: Morris Plains, p. 56-67

Jaquet-Chiffelle, D.-O. et al. (2009). "Virtual Persons and Identities". In: Rannenberg et al. (ed.) *The Future of Identity in the Information Society: Challenges and Opportunities*. Berlin: Springer Verlag, p. 75-122.

Jarvis, J. L. (2014, June 2). "Digital image politics: the networked rhetoric of Anonymous". In: Global Discourse: An Interdisciplinary Journal of Current Affairs and Applied Contemporary Thought. Volume 4, Issue 2-3, 2014, p. 326-49.

Kneale, J. (2006, January 1). "From beyond: H. P. Lovecraft and the place of horror". In: *Cultural Geographies 2006, 13*, p. 106-26.

Kohns, O. (2013). Guy Fawkes in the 21st century. A contribution to the political iconography of revolt. In: *Image & Narrative, 14(1), 2013*, p. 89-104.

Lewis, C. S. (1969). *An Experiment in Criticism*. Cambridge: Cambridge University Press.

Murray, C. (2002). "Popaganda: Superhero Comics and Propaganda in World War Two". In: Magnussen & Christiansen (ed.) *Comics Culture: Analytical and Theoretical Approaches to Comics*. Copenhagen: Museum Tusculanum Press, p. 141-56.

Nail, T. (2013). "Zapatismo and the Global Origins of Occupy". In: *JCRT 12.3 Spring 2013*, p. 20-37.

Olson, P. (2012). We Are Anonymous: Inside the Hacker World of LulzSec, Anonymous, and the Global Cyber Insurgency. New York, NY: Little, Brown and Company.

Paget, F. (2012). Hacktivism: Cyberspace has become the new medium of political Voices. White Paper by McAfee, p. 1-34.

Parkin, L. (2011). *Alan Moore*. Harpenden: OldCastle Books.

Peterson, J. (2012). Playing at the World: A History of Simulating Wars, People and Fantastic Adventures from Chess to Role-Playing Games. San Diego: Unreason Press.

Pittaway, J. (2012). "Identifying Anonymous". In: Swan (ed.) *On the Cyber*. Raleigh, NC: Lulu, p. 73-82.

Raymond, E. S. (2000). "A Brief History of Hackerdom". In: DiBona et al. (ed.) *Open Sources*. http://www.immagic.com/eLibrary/ARCHIVES/GENERAL/AUTHOR_P/R000825P.pdf

Rosen, J. (2012). "The People Formerly Known as the audience". In: Mandiberg (ed.) *The Social Media Reader*. New York, NY: New York University Press.

Rosenweig, R. (1998, December). "Wizards, Bureaucrats, Warriors, and Hackers: Writing the History of the Internet". In: *The American Historical Review, Vol. 103, No. 5 (Dec., 1998)*, p. 1530-52.

Sanders, J. (1994). *Science Fiction Fandom*. Westport, CT: Greenwood Press.

Schelly, B. (2002). Founders of Comic Fandom: Profiles of 90 Publishers, Dealers, Collectors, Writers, Artists and Other Luminaries of the 1950s and 1960s. Seattle: Hamster Press.

Shifman, L. (2014). *Memes in Digital Culture*. Cambridge, Mass.: The MIT Press

Spencer, T. S. (1957). *The History of Amateur Journalism*. New York, NY: The Fossils.

Stryker, C. (2011). Epic Win for Anonymous: How 4chan's Army Conquered the Web. New York, NY: Overlook Duckworth.

Tolkien, J. R. R. (1997). "On Fairy-Stories". In: Tolkien (ed.) *The Monsters & the Critics and Other Essays*. London: HarperCollins Publ., p. 109-61.

Documentation

churchofscientology (2008, January 21). "Message to Scientology". http://www.youtube.com/watch?v=JCbKv9yiLiQ

Gray, R. (2011, November 22). "Shepard Fairey Changes Unpopular 'Occupy Hope' Poster Under Pressure". In: *The Village Voice Blogs Tue., Nov. 22 2011*. http://blogs.villagevoice.com/runninscared/2011/11/shepard_fairey_6.php

Lamont, T. (2011, November 26). "Alan Moore – meet the man behind the protest mask". In: *The Observer, Saturday 26 November 2011.* http://www.theguardian.com/books/2011/nov/27/alan-moore-v-vendetta-mask-protest

LaughingOutLol (2011, August 8). "[VOSTFR] Message from Anonymous : Operation Facebook, Nov 5 2011". http://www.youtube.com/watch?v=Q6crH8qmyZ8

Moore, A. (2012, February 10). "Viewpoint: V for Vendetta and the rise of Anonymous". In: *BBC News, February 10, 2012.* http://www.bbc.co.uk/news/technology-16968689

Solon, O. (2012, July 4). "Acta la vista, baby! European Parliament rejects controversial trade agreement". In: *Wired.co.uk, July 4th 2012.* http://www.wired.co.uk/news/archive/2012-07/04/acta-dead

TheAlyonaShow (2011, August 10). "'Operation Facebook' Hack or Hoax?". http://www.youtube.com/watch?v=24zvr-0_XCs

Warman, M. (2012, January 27). "Europe signs up to controversial ACTA web treaty". In: *The Telegraph, January 27, 2012.* http://www.telegraph.co.uk/technology/news/9044699/Europe-signs-up-to-controversial-ACTA-web-treaty.html

Private Bodies, Public Pleasures: Asserting Male Dominance through Internet Creepshots

Kristen Colbeck

Abstract: This paper explores the recent online photographic phenomenon of creepshots, examining the implications of this trend psychoanalytically. Creepshots are non-consensual photographs taken of women in public spaces, shared online via forums for the express purposes of sexual gratification. The objective of this paper is two-fold. First, the author outlines the parameters for understanding the significance of these photographs as a categorically fetishistic perversion (fetishistic scopophilia), as they serve a predominately visual pleasure function. However, the author also argues that this fetishism works in conjunction with voyeuristic scopophilia, arguing against Mulvey's (2009b) contention that the male audience will choose one or the other for dealing with female visual objects. By subjecting women to voyeuristic and fetishistic scopophilia, it is argued that creepshot producers and consumers subconsciously and anonymously work to symbolically remove power from their female subjects, reducing them to passive sexual objects for widespread male domination and consumption.

Keywords: Feminist media studies, psychoanalysis, Internet voyeurism, Reddit, creepshots.

Introduction

"When you are in public, you do not have a reasonable expectation of privacy. We kindly ask women to respect our right to admire your bodies and stop complaining" (Valenti, 2013a, p.6). So said the introduction to a forum on "social news" website Reddit devoted to an alarming photographic trend called creepshots. A creepshot can be defined as "non-consensual pictures of women snapped in public places" (p.6). The purpose of these photographs is sexual in nature, with the preferred subject being a fit woman in tightly-fitted clothing. To emphasize the purpose of these photographs, the caption of one particular photo speaks volumes: "get yur [sic] tissues!! Insane beach bubble butt" (p.6), the photo's poster proclaims.

With the vast quantity and varying genres of often free pornography available on the Internet, it is clear that there is more to these creepshots than just sex. What perpetuates the production and consumption of creepshots is not only the physical attractiveness of the women they depict, but also the implications they have of both power and control over their female subjects. This is especially true if one considers the latter part of the introduction provided by the creepshot purveyors of Reddit, wherein it is implicit "a woman's right to protect her body is overruled by a man's desire to view it" (Valenti, 2013b).

The deeper implications of the production and consumption of these images can be understood psychoanalytically, and it is clear that this specific appropriation of women's images is two-fold: an unrestricted gaze onto a female subject that supplants the sexual act itself, while also suppressing power in the female subject. Women are permitted a more masculine/active approach to their identities and their sexuality than ever before, as supported by changes in western laws and attitudes from the 1960s to the present-day. A woman can say no; she now has sexual power not previously held, creating a tension between "instinctual drives and self-preservation" (Mulvey, 2009, p.19) in men. This tension is the feeling of sexual attraction countered by a threat to masculinity. By subjecting women to voyeuristic and fetishistic scopophilia, creepshot producers and consumers subconsciously work to symbolically remove power from their female subjects. This is achieved by forcing them into a sexual experience without their consent or knowledge, into a situation where they cannot say no or protest this act. Creepshot producers and consumers, while achieving sexual satisfaction through the fetishization of the female, simultaneously achieve satisfaction by symbolically asserting dominance and control over women.

Justifying the creepshot?

While creepshots are not a core part of academic discourse more generally, they have been the focus of many articles within the pages of feminist magazines such as Bitch, Ms., and online feminist-oriented social news site Jezebel. Articles pertaining to the topic typically attribute the rise of creepshots to the Reddit community, as well as the increasing laissez-faire attitude western culture has to mobile photography via smartphones. However, the issue of voyeurism – of which creepshots are certainly a subcategory within – is not new. As Draeger (2011) points out: if *"prostitution is [...] the oldest profession"* then *"voyeurism may be the oldest pastime"* (p.41).

Speaking specifically to a briefer historiography of voyeurism, it seems most appropriate to compare the creepshot voyeurs of the Internet age to the classical notion of the Peeping Tom. The roots of the modern-day Peeping Tom come from the legend of Lady Godiva and her infamous nude ride. According to this legend, the Lady confronts her husband – the cruel and unpassionate ruler of Coventry – about reducing the taxes on the peasantry of their town (Ellis Davidson, 1969, p.109). He agrees to alleviate the tax on the condition that she rides naked through their town on horseback, under the assumption that her modesty will make her refuse (p.109). She indeed agrees to this proposition, but prior to her ride has a herald announce that *"from then till noon no foot should pace the street, no eye look down...but that all should keep within, door shut, and window barr'd"* (Tennyson, in

Draeger, p.42). All obey this command except for one unrestrained tailor called Tom, whose curiosity gets the better of him and against the Lady's wishes, takes a peek as she rides by (Ellis Davidson, p.116). Peeping Tom, now the most infamous voyeur, is instantly blinded when he spies out his window in some stories, while in other versions he actually dies as a result of his disobedience (p.117).

Peeping Tom raises an interesting query about the possibility of voyeurism's harm. Lady Godiva made clear her desire to not be watched, and as a noblewoman, this request obviously hit its target with the rest of town. She was not merely a naked woman parading through town, but a hierarchically more significant person whose presence demanded respect and obedience. To contrast Draeger's (2011) argument, there is no room in this instance to understand Tom's punishment as a result of violation of social norms or his peering to be the result of gender asymmetries – the harm committed is violation of the will of power, and is civil disobedience in its strangest form. Tom's failure to adhere to this significant distinction between a common woman and a nobleperson ultimately results in his punishment, as he has harmed Godiva through the violation of her request as a nobleperson to not be looked upon.

By establishing the parameters for harm, Tom – real or not – has assisted the voyeurs of today to continue to justify their peeping, as there seems to be a clinging to the claim that there is no harm done. This dialogue has consistently appeared throughout the defenses of the producers and consumers of creepshots, particularly by way of pointing out that these acts are perfectly legal, and of course alluding to the aforementioned unreasonableness of expecting personal privacy in public spaces. There seems a constant latent underscoring of the notion that these women are not "special", apart from their physical attractiveness, and therefore deserve no "special treatment". They are not Lady Godiva, they do not have the power of nobility, they did not individually ask to not be photographed, and there can consequently be no harm done to them and no reasonable retribution in return.

There is no threat of blindness or death onto the Peeping Toms of the Internet age for these abovementioned justifications, but also because of the relative safety of the medium itself. Having a computer screen as a barrier between looker and looked upon protects the looker from scrutiny for their act of voyeurism. While the individuals taking the photographs risk getting caught, to which they have broken social norms of looking, those who are simply viewing the photographs have the safety of both their relative Internet anonymity, as well as the viewing confines of their own home. An interesting irony, indeed, that privacy is taken from a woman to become a private moment for a man.

The safety of the viewing environment allows for an unrestricted gaze free of time constraints or social boundaries – the looker has free reign of his subject akin to spectators at the zoo, keenly staggered around the lion's enclosure, aware of its power but reassured by a formidable fence. There is no shame; there is no reprimand. Like the child gazing onto another, curious of the unknown bodily *"otherness"* of that differently sexed person, the creepshot aficionados exercise their paraphilic curiosity unrestrained. Creepshots allow for a new freedom in sexual voyeuristic fetishism, in spite of the fact that *"basic bodily contours are no mystery"* (Draeger, p.44). This perversion apparent in creepshots is very clearly identified as scopophilic, both fetishistic and voyeuristic, and its implications may be discussed theoretically through Mulvey (2009b), though its foundations are found in Freud (2011).

Freud and Perversions

Freud (2011) describes scopophilia, or more simply *"pleasure in looking"* (p.35), as a form of sexual aberration, or perversion, wherein the act of looking substitutes an actual sexual object in deriving pleasure. Perversions take on two forms. First, they can be sexual activities that extend beyond the typical anatomy intended for sexual activity, the genitals (p. 28), and secondly, they can manifest in the form of a prolonged lingering upon the sexual excitations that lead to the final act of copulation (p. 28).

A suitable sexual object under these conditions might be something like the hair or feet of a sexual partner, overlooking the sexual partner to focus specifically on these features for pleasure. In a full fetishistic condition, something like the colour of a partner's hair or a specific bodily condition may constitute necessary means for achieving sexual fulfillment. In this situation, the fetish in question is no longer a condition necessary of a partner, like in the fetish of a particular hair colour, but is actually the sole sexual object (p.33). For these individuals, sexual pleasure is not derived from a partner who possesses or embodies their fetish, but is actually derived from the fetish itself.

Freud posits that, like the tactile sensation of touching – which is an inherent part of the normal excitations preceding sexual union – visual impressions are too a *"pathway along which libidinal excitation is aroused"* (p.35). Furthermore, the covering and concealing of the body maintains a sexual curiosity, stimulating the excitation of revealing such hidden parts of the body. This excitation, going above and beyond the normal parameters of sexual interest, is thus known as scopophilia. The specifics of scopophilia detail it as a fetish or perversion once this act of looking is focused solely on the genitals, or with a focus on the acts of excretion/micturition, as in voyeurs. It also becomes perverse once, as described above, it supplants its purpose as an excitation with being the sole sexual aim.

Love of Looking, Love of Self

What is notable about scopophilia is the level of narcissism that is initially involved in the desire and love to look. As Baranger (1991) points out, in scopophilia the initial subject of the look is an individual's own body, providing immense autoerotic satisfaction in the beginnings of mental life (p.113). This narcissism and scopophilia is also associated with sadism and masochism. Sadism, the more aggressive and active of the two, involves the control over a sexual object for satisfaction, and is potentially the remnants of the primordial drive for total mastery (Freud, 2011). This may include bringing pain to a partner, maltreating, or humiliating them. Given its aggressiveness, Freud consigns sadism to the realm of masculinity, stating men are more likely to employ aggression for sexual satisfaction (p.36). In a struggle to maintain and preserve the ego, hate is exacted in relation to objects external from the self to reinforce the love for oneself – to reinforce and maintain the narcissism inherent in the sadist (Baranger, p.126).

Control and destructiveness satisfies the ego's narcissistic need for omnipotence (p.127). This privileging of the needs of the self over that of the will of the partner for sexual satisfaction is tied to the ego, and is certainly apparent in the solely self-serving nature of creepshots.

The relative ignorance for the other present in the narcissistic sadist perhaps has its foundations in the male child, who is keenly aware of his own genitalia. As Freud notes, little boys attribute their own genitalia to everyone they know, and the absence of a penis among the individuals in their world is unimaginable. However, such ignorance does not last forever, and upon witnessing the absence of a penis for females, male children face internal struggle such as the infamous castration complex. This complex assumes, for both sexes, that at some point females did have a penis but somehow lost it, whether through their own folly or otherwise. Freud notes that this creates an *"enduringly low opinion"* of females by males, and is a great determining factor in males' perversions (p.73). This privileging of maleness, in contrast with the lacking in femaleness, marginalizes the female and creates an intense curiosity and paranoia surrounding her physique. The male gaze onto the female, as will be discussed, serves to quell the paranoia and curiosity, while also asserting pleasurable control.

Mulvey and Voyeuristic and Fetishistic Scopophilia

Mulvey (2009b) famously builds upon Freud's ideas of both scopophilia and narcissism, assuming a highly patriarchal, phallocentric society, with male as standard and female as deviation. This phallocentrism is highly dependent on the lack of a penis in the female – the so- called "castrated woman" – to provide overall structure and meaning to the world. Due to this perceived lacking, the castrated female assists in bolstering the symbolic power of the penis and therefore also of the men who possess it. The female is relegated to only the bearer of this *"bleeding wound"* – the vagina – existing only in relation to it and never transcending its meaning (p.15). She is not the maker of meaning, but only the bearer of it, acting as the signifier of the male "other" and bound by his symbolic power. In this patriarchal order, females are the *"silent image"* tied and subject to the fantasies and obsessions of males (p.15).

The Pleasure – and Narcissism – in Looking

Speaking specifically about film, Mulvey claims that current representations of females are largely unchallenged, with the normal pleasurable expectations of film guided by the language of the dominant patriarchal order (p.16). Erotic pleasure in film is centred on the image of the woman, which works to satisfy and reinforce the masculine ego in two ways. First, this is in the form of pleasurable looking, but also in the narcissistic fascination with identifying with on-screen male heroes. In the realm of the cinema, scopophilia is facilitated via the isolating darkness of an auditorium, which separates spectators from one another, and also on the screen, where the movie's shifting patterns of light and dark masquerade as voyeuristic separation. The cinema's spectators, according to Mulvey, are repressed in their exhibitionism and love of looking, and this repressed desire is projected onto the film's performers through the active male and passive female.

It may seem surprising that both the male and female actors are used for the purposes of viewing pleasure, but their roles are starkly contrasted. While the female is used as the object of the gaze, and is constructed with a certain "to-be-looked-at-ness", the male is employed as a representation of the self, and is the controller of the visual scene. The audience identifies with and therefore reflect themselves onto the male, controlling the film fantasy and maintaining representative power – they are the bearer of the look and meaning, driving the narrative forward. This identification with the male power develops scopophilia into its narcissistic aspect.

The Process of Female Neutralization

The nature in which the neutralization of the female occurs is of the greatest interest in this work, because the female form actually poses a deep, latent problem for the male gaze. As aforementioned, because the female lacks a penis, she is viewed as a castrated individual. In the absence of her penis she acts as a reminder of the threat of castration, dissolving the idea of pleasure. So although she is the passive recipient of the male gaze, she also represents his castration anxiety. Neutralizing this anxiety in the male unconscious is fundamental for the security and continuance of male pleasure, and Mulvey (2009b) posits that this nullification manifests in two forms. First, the female can be *"investigated"* to uncover the original trauma of her castration, which is then counterbalanced by either her devaluation, punishment or saving.

Her castration can also be cast aside altogether, with a substitution for the penis being found in a reassuring fetish object. In her work *"Fear, Fantasy, and the Male Unconscious"* (2009a), Mulvey describes these replacements as phallic fetishes as *"shoes, corsets, rubber gloves, belts, knickers and so on – which serve as signs for the lost penis but have no direct connection with it"* (p.11). This replacement can also be the transforming of the female into a fetish herself – an overvaluation, as in the cult of the female superstar (Mulvey, 2009b, p.22).

This sadistic control of the female, with its desire to view and uncover in an effort to make sound judgement, is thusly termed voyeuristic scopophilia. As Mulvey (2009b) states, its pleasure is derived from *"ascertaining guilt [...] asserting control, and subjugating the guilty person through punishment or forgiveness"* (p.22). Its counterpart, and the other method for which the male unconscious will neutralize the female castration threat, is fetishistic scopophilia. Fetishistic scopophilia involves building up the physical beauty of the threat, and as such transforming it into satisfaction in and of itself. Unlike the sadism of voyeuristic scopophilia, which works quite well to bolster a film's narrative, fetishistic scopophilia "exists outside linear time" as it is focused alone on an eroticized gaze and the pleasure in looking (p.22).

Voyeuristic and Fetishistic Scopophilia in Creepshots

The Internet has a unique privilege for facilitating scopophilia. Though not quite as capable of reproducing the "so-called natural conditions of human perception" (p.21) that film offers, the Internet and immersive technologies increasingly find ways of structuring a limitless screen space wherein everything becomes real. The actual, technical look is forgotten in an effort to create a real world wherein an on-screen surrogate is ultimately believable. There is no detachment to visibly ascertain – the Internet audience is the "invisible guest" wherever they venture to. Of course, for creepshots, a computer screen mediates viewership and allows for seamless entanglement of audience and surrogate, combining voyeuristic with fetishistic scopophilia.

Creepshots make use of both types of scopophilia in tandem in an effort to neutralize the castration anxiety brought upon by the female subjects in the photos, and thus opposes Mulvey's argument where male spectators will employ one or the other. Fetishism of the female subject can act as a front or protective excuse for voyeuristic – and sadistic – scopophilia to flourish.

Neutralizing the female threat in this mode goes beyond just age old castration anxiety, and is actually a method of removing the sexual power of the female and returning her to the passive state dictated to her by the confines of patriarchy. In the realm of both Freud and Mulvey, as is certainly veritable in the online realm, penis is king – not possessing this source of symbolic power and yet acting in an active/male way is simply unacceptable.

Fetishizing the Object, Neutralizing the Subject

As suggested, fetishistic scopophilia is first employed as a means of justifying the creation and viewing of these images. Fetishism of the female form is, as Mulvey suggests, the status quo – women exist on screen for the viewing pleasure of men, and off screen they function in the same way. This is their place in the patriarchal pecking order. The foundation of this fetishistic viewing exists through visual media such as film or photography, wherein it is obvious that the purpose of the female image is to provide visual pleasure. This constant display of female as object has solidified and normalized her role in the world, making it acceptable to continually produce her likeness in this way. This is why creepshots appear to pose no issue to the male creators and viewers, because in reality they are no different in content than how women are represented in other visual media. The image of the female, though entirely unglamorous in most of these photos, holds the public function of providing visual pleasure to the male audience. Her likeness – not as an individual person, but as a woman-object – is fetishized in the real world by the male who views her. Subsequently, if he deems her image to be good enough, he can claim her or own her by enshrining her in a photograph – he can continue to fetishize her form beyond that singular moment and may choose to share his bounty with others.

The fetishized gaze in this particular branch of Mulvey's two types of scopophilia aligns best with Freud's detailing of scopophilia as a perversion. For Freud, scopophilia is the desire to look but the knowledge that this is not morally or socially acceptable. Staring or gawking at another person in public for a prolonged period is still unacceptable, and warrants concern about the individual doing the staring. There is a negative connotation attached with a person transfixing their gaze on a stranger, especially when it is a male looking upon a female. Perhaps the female desire to not be looked at finds its roots in the tale of Lady Godiva, but more likely stems from the innate need for privacy that most adults feel – the right to be "left alone" that is a naturally understood part of interaction, but seems to not exist for women when it is inconvenient for men.

Warren and Brandeis (1890) provide a definition that recognizes the various aspects that encompass a right to privacy. They state that all individuals have *"the right to enjoy life, -- the right to be let alone; the right to liberty secures the exercise of extensive civil privileges"*, while *"the term "property" has grown to comprise every form of possession -- intangible, as well as tangible"* (p.193). Physical access to a person is certainly a feature of this definition, and yet it is physical access that is violated in the process of snapping a creepshot – of course, this is just one among the thrills that are sought after.

Perhaps this can assist in explaining why such a trend in photography has burst in popularity on the Internet, in spite of the vast quantities of women's candid photographs on social networking sites, in addition to the amount of free pornography available. Self-snapped photos are not truly voyeuristic, with the female not sufficiently pacified to provide pleasure from domination. In something like a self-posted photograph, the female subject is not *"hetero- sexy"* (Shields Dobson, p.5) enough. In her work, Shields Dobson (2010) notes that the "selfies" posted to photo-sharing websites often depict females in an active/male fashion. They strike vulgar, sexualized poses, mouths open and hands gesturing aggressively. These women are not passive image objects for viewing, and more importantly, they are aware of the camera's presence as both subject and operator, posing specifically for its eye, as well as for themselves. It is for this same reason that pornography does not work explicitly to satisfy this perversion. For Freud, scopophilia replaces the physical sex partner or object with the sole abstraction of looking as the source of sexual satisfaction. Pornography is itself a sex object, and is intended quite plainly for the purposes of sexual pleasure – the genitals are on display, thus the mystery of the body and the thrill of *"sneaking a peak"* does not exist. As a perversion, scopophilia sexualizes the non-sexual act of looking. Perhaps this can explain why the subjects of the majority of creepshots are depicted in strangely unsexual situations, such as waiting in queue at the supermarket check-out or walking through a university campus.

Voyeurism and Sadism in the Gaze

While the patriarchal normalization of female fetishization may make the photography of unknowing and unwilling females seem fairly innocent, it acts only as a mask for the greater purposes of these photographs – to bring about feelings of control over the subject. Hence voyeuristic scopophilia is the true aim and pleasure in these photographs.

Why might a creator or viewer of this type of photography want to feel control or power in this way? Beyond the castration anxiety attached to females, there may also be spitefulness towards her active/masculine sexuality – which is a brazen defiance of the patriarchal order – either brought on by or in combination with male self-perceived (sexual) inadequacy. Female sexuality has certainly blossomed in recent decades. Since the second wave of feminism in the 1960's, in combination with advancements in contraceptive measures, women have gained more control over their sexual lives and well-being. Far from the structures of traditional, oppressive *"femininity,"* women now enjoy more sexual freedom than previously permitted, thus aligning themselves more so with masculinity.

For Freud, the idea that a woman can enjoy a pleasure-driven sexuality is quite foreign, with the complete absence of an erotic or desirous state actually considered to be a distinctly feminine attribute (Hoffman, 1999). Furthermore, Freud posits that women necessarily dampen all desires to develop normal femininity, and a woman's aggression/masculinity must be avoided to prove to a potential male partner that she is able to both repress and be repressed (p.145).

Masculinity is therefore aligned with active sexuality, and pursuing and initiating sexual relations belongs within the realm of the masculine. He gives and she receives, of course in strict anatomical terms, but also in social expectations. With women's liberation, this strict binary of power is distorted as women assume a masculinized sexuality which is as threatening to masculinity as the absence of her penis, and therefore must be counteracted.

Secondary to the threat of the masculinized and powerful women is the meaning that this presents for the self-perceived power of the male. If a woman has as much sexual power and self-ownership as she does without a penis, a man may wonder what this says about him as male with a penis, especially if he is not sexually confident. As West (2013) suggests, women who are sexually empowered are often the target of male scrutiny because of their own self-perceived inadequacies and perceived inability to control their own lives. Furthermore, West (2013) posits that men transfix their attention to non-consensual sexual advancements onto women because if it is consensual *"it's "sluttiness," and sluttiness is agency and agency is threatening"* (n.p.).

While the women in the candid creepshot photographs are not entirely glamorous, they are also not entirely unsexual. The subjects of these photographs are typically wearing tight or revealing clothing, and are often in bathing suits at the beach or a pool – they are relaxed in their state of dress and unaware. This provides male purveyors of these photos with a two-fold opportunity. First, they have the chance to submit their object to a non-consensual situation and revel in her sexualized state, satisfying fetishistic scopophilia. Second, they also get to appeal to their ego by shaming her for her manner of dress or her body, such as one commenter who states: *"Backpack is ugly but everything else is beautiful"* (fashionBen, 2013). Another poster, commenting on an attractive woman in a sheer dress, sarcastically asks *"Is her hair that sloppy on purpose?!"* (nolpek, 2013). The same commenter, on a different photo mocks the subject matter, stating *"um, ew? That could be a man for all we know"* (nolpek, 2013). One commenter, on a photograph of a woman at the gym, declares *"[t]hat ass is to [sic] flat for yoga pants"* (Trick901, 2013).

This sadistic tendency for judgment is noted in Mulvey (2009b, p. 22), but it is Freud (2011) that more effectively explains this as a feature of masculinity. Freud points out the male need to subjugate, maltreat or humiliate the object for pleasure (p. 36). He explains that this control by overcoming a sexual object by means *"other than the process of wooing"* (p. 36) is an aggressive feature of male sexuality. By acting out this process of male sadistic, voyeuristic scopophilia, wherein they are free to judge and comment on the female object, male creepshot creators and viewers reaffirm their masculinity and mastery over females. By scrutinizing the subject and declaring if she is worth a *"fap"* or not (masturbation), they stimulate voyeuristic scopophilia, and symbolically neutralize their female object as a threat by returning her to only a state of passive sexuality.

Facilitating Access, Enabling Control

The reason that this is at all possible is thanks to the mode in which it is displayed, which is much like the cinematic experience that Mulvey (2009b) describes. Like in the auditorium, each individual sitting alone at his computer screen experiences the voyeuristic separation between himself and the object of his gaze. He experiences a similar *"on-screen"* surrogate, and while the surrogate is not a part of the image, he is the eye of the image and controls the gaze.

Both time and space are frozen, subordinated to meet his needs – the union between spectator and surrogate are indeed seamless. Furthermore, he is supported and reinforced in his role as spectator via his community of like-minded voyeurs, who encourage and legitimize this conduct as normal and acceptable. The spectator can come in direct contact with his surrogate

146

and delve deeper into the condition of the object – what was she doing, where was she going, how much or how little does the surrogate know about her – to further satisfy his fetishization of her.

Simultaneously, the surrogate who has taken and posted this photo also reinforces this gaze by reaffirming the lack of harm in taking such photos. As one creepshot poster states: *"If these lovely young women CHOOSE to dress in clothes that guys like to look at, in public, then, they have no reasonable expectation of privacy, and taking a pic that does not identify the person, is NO DIFFERENT than taking a mental picture"* (luv2race, 2013). Another attempts to replace the creepiness of the photos by likening them to fashion critiques only, stating *"[j]ust trying to offer fashion commentary. These ladies are in public. Nothing wrong here at all."* (can-diddly, 2013).

The attitude that women in public do not deserve special treatment or to treated with dignity harkens back to the earlier discussion of Lady Godiva. Peeping Tom was punishable because it is made explicit from the Lady herself that she was not to be looked upon. Her position as nobility made her request deadly to ignore, even when her state of undress seemed to invite curiosity. In the male creepshot mind, their female subjects have not gone out of their way to say no, and their manner of dress may even appear to be an invitation to gawk. If they are not *"special"*, there is no reason for them to be protected– as reiterated time and again on sites such as Reddit. A woman in public is akin to a buck in hunting season – she is fair game to be captured and owned with the click of a camera.

Like Mulvey's (2009b) voyeuristic film audience, the viewers at each computer screen who perpetuate the victimization of creepshot subjects are *"lulled into a false sense of security by the apparent legality of his surrogate"* (p.25). It is reiterated that there is no legal problem behind these photographs, and that the women ought to be flattered by the attention they receive, as if a favour is being done for them. When attempts are made to highlight the indecency and inappropriateness of the creepshots, the photographs' connoisseurs are quick to jump to their defense and shamelessly insult those who would oppose them. When one user asks *"wonder how she would feel if she knew you were taking sneaky photos of her... Would she be ok with it or think you a slimeball"* (J0HNN0, 2013), another user is quick to reply *"dude you're on the wrong [forum] for giving a shit... go home"* (mysticalmisogynistic, 2013). With very few voices directly responding to the invasiveness of these photographs and a community of like-minded males encouraging this activity, a safe environment is fostered for these males to use the images on unknowing, *"insignificant"* women to boost their egos while simultaneously visually – and therefore sexually – pleasing themselves.

However even the *"significant"* women – celebrities or women in positions of power – are not safe from the repercussions of fetishistic and voyeuristic scopophilia. For example, in late August 2014, hundreds of nude self-photographs of young female celebrities such as Kate Upton and Mary Elizabeth Winstead were stolen and released online on sites such as Reddit and 4Chan in an event known widely as either *"The Fappening"* or *"CelebGate"*. While one victim, Jennifer Lawrence, stated explicitly that what occurred was a sex crime, one user on the Reddit page (subreddit) dedicated to sharing the photographs justified the release, stating *"...everyone is so quick to attribute the interest [in the nude photographs] to some misogynistic perversion, but it's really just human nature"* (Johnson, 2014). This event closely aligns with creepshots and the trend of *"revenge porn"*, where nude photographs shared privately with a former sexual and/or romantic partner are released online after the dissolution of the relationship, as a form of retribution for the ending of the relationship. The attitude, it seems, that stems from these online photographic trends is that if women do not want their nude photographs *"leaked"* online, then they should not take them in the first place, again shifting the blame and shame onto the

148

victims instead of the perpetrators who remain safely anonymous behind usernames and computer screens.

Conclusion

Though there have been numerous backlashes against creepshots and many successful shutdowns of forums and websites hosting creepshot photographs, this phenomenon has not been completely eradicated. Each time a forum is closed another pops up in its place. On Reddit, which originally host a forum specifically called creepshots, a replacement forum emerged under the title "*Candid Fashion Police*", claiming to be a place for "*people post candid photos of women and then we judge their fashion choices similar to TLC's what not to wear and E!'s FashionPolice*" (Reddit.com, 2013). In reality, this was just another forum to post creepshots, and as such has since been taken down.

There is more to the creepshot phenomenon than just "*appreciating*" women's beauty. Though the entire phenomenon is maintained under the guise of fetishistic scopophilia, wherein the beauty of the object is built up and is fetishized, creepshots are actually a façade for the larger purpose of sadistic, voyeuristic scopophilia. The latter works well to neutralize the threat to men posed by female castration and free sexuality, and by capturing and judging the female subjects of these photographs, the male spectators assert control and ownership over them. They are empowered by subjecting their female objects to unwanted and unconsented sexual attention, narcissistically answering to only their own needs while they disregard the rights of the person depicted in the photograph. In the static patriarchal rape culture of western society, wherein the objectification of women is a standard, saying nothing is unfortunately perceived as being an equivalent to consent.

The termination of creepshots is not possible without a radical shifting in the way in which women are visually represented in media and the attitudes that surround these depictions. So long as media such as film and television employ the image of a female as a spectacle for looking at, or her image as a vehicle for male storytelling, then it is hardly possible to convince the male minds of the world that it is not okay to similarly use the image of a woman for their own needs. The outcomes of Web 2.0 and convergence practices present a frontier to be conquered in both the theory and praxis of feminism – one that is, like the abovementioned media, predominately made for men and by men. As Mulvey (2009a) states, the image of woman "*has continually [been] stolen and used*" (p.27) for male pleasure within these media, but the solution for ending this assumption of ownership is certainly not one found in merely asking for hosting websites to remove these creepshots or pointing out the nature of their invasiveness. There is no way to produce an alternative "*out of the blue*", but as Mulvey posits, breakthroughs can be made by examining patriarchy using its own tools, among which critical psychoanalytic assessment of our images and visual practices "*is not the only [tool] but an important one*" (p.15).

References

Baranger, W. (1991). Narcissism in Freud. In J. Sandler, E. Spector Person, & P. Fonagy (Eds.), *Freud's 'on narcissism: an introduction'* (pp. 108-130). New Haven, CT: Yale University Press.

Draeger, J. (2011). What peeping tom did wrong. *Ethic Theory and Moral Practice, 14*(1), 41- 49.

Ellis Davidson, H. R. (1969). The legend of lady Godiva. *Folklore, 80*(2), 107-121.

Freud, S. (2011). *Three essays on the theory of sexuality*. (J. Strachey, Trans.) Mansfield Centre, CT: Martino Publishing. (Original work published 1949).

Hoffman, L. (1999). Focusing on active sexuality in women. In D. Bassin (Ed.), *Female sexuality: contemporary engagements* (pp. 141-152). Northvale, NJ: Jason Aronson, Inc.

Mulvey, L. (2009a). Fears, fantasies, and the male unconscious or 'you don't know what is happening, do you, Mr. Jones?'. In *Visual and other pleasures* (pp. 6-13). New York, NY: Palgrave MacMillan.

Mulvey, L. (2009b). Visual pleasure and narrative cinema. In *Visual and other pleasures* (pp. 14 27). New York, NY: Palgrave MacMillan.

Shields Dobson, A. (2008). The 'grotesque body' in young women's self-presentation on MySpace. In *Australian Sociological Association Conference: Re-Imagining Society, Melbourne.*

Valenti, M. (2013a, Fall). Phone freaks keep on creepin' on. *Bitch, 18*(60), 6.

Warren, S.D. & Brandeis, L.D. (1890). The right to privacy. *Harvard Law Review, 4*(5), 193- 220.

Documentation

can-diddly. (2013, December 13). What an ugly backpack! [Forum comment]. Message posted to:
http://www.reddit.com/r/CandidFashionPolice/comments/1seb63/what _an_ugly_backpa k/

fashionBen. (2013, December 10). What an ugly backpack! [Forum comment]. Message posted to:
http://www.reddit.com/r/CandidFashionPolice/comments/1seb63/what _an_ugly_back pack/

J0HNN0. (2013, December 15). Honestly you look great [Forum comment]. Message posted to:
http://www.reddit.com/r/CandidFashionPolice/comments/1szwjp/hones tly_you_look_gr at/

Johnson, E.M. (2014, September 24). Misogyny is not human nature. *Slate.* Retrieved from:

http://www.slate.com/articles/health_and_science/science/2014/09/online_misogyny_of_the_fappening_stealing_celebrity_photos_is_not_just_human.htm

luv2race. (2013, December 12). What an ugly backpack! [Forum comment]. Message posted to http://www.reddit.com/r/CandidFashionPolice/comments/1seb63/what_an_ugly_backpack/mysticalmisogynistic. (2013, December 15). Honestly you look great [Forum comment]. Message posted to http://www.reddit.com/r/CandidFashionPolice/comments/1szwjp/honestly_you_look_gr at/

nolpek. (2013, December 5). Good job going all white but this dress is a bit too see through to wear in public [Forum comment]. Message posted to: http://www.reddit.com/r/CandidFashionPolice/comments/1s2ofk/good_job_going_all_w ite_but_this_dress_is_a_bit/

nolpek. (2013, December 5). Nice pocket design. Bag seems too full [Forum comment]. Message posted to: http://www.reddit.com/r/CandidFashionPolice/comments/1rmorp/nice_pocket_design_bag_seems_too_full/

Reddit.com (2013). *CandidFashionPolice*. Retrieved from: http://www.reddit.com/r/CandidFashionPolice/

SchuminWeb. (2013, December 16). Cowboy boots and one piece cupcake-patterned pajamas [Forum comment]. Message posted to http://www.reddit.com/r/CandidFashionPolice/comments/1sxsni/cowboy_boots_and_on_piece_cupcakepatterned/

Valenti, M. (2013b, June 12). Creepshots: are you being creeped on? [Web log post]. Retrieved from: http://msmagazine.com/blog/2013/06/12/creepshots-are-you-being-creeped-on/

West, L. (2013, May 7). Female 'purity' is bullshit. [Web log post]. Retrieved from: http://jezebel.com/female-purity-is-bullshit-493278191

An Hero and the Trolls

Lars Konzack

Abstract: This is an investigation into the case of Mitchell Henderson seen in the light of heroes and villains. The MySpace page commemorating Hendersons suicide was subject to a form of activity known as "trolling", of such intensity that Henderson became an iconic figure, a "meme" in the troll community known as "Anonymous." Examination of this singular event leads eventually to a wider discussion of what it means to be a hero and whether or not Anonymous should be considered villains, heroes, tricksters or vigilantes. Furthermore, it attempts an understanding of what Anonymous are, how they operate, and insight into their distinctive Internet culture.

Keywords: Anonymous, 4chan, An Hero Day, Trolls, Tricksters, Vigilantes, Mitchell Henderson.

Introduction

Researching an Internet culture such as Anonymous is difficult, due to the fact that they are, indeed, anonymous. Nonetheless it has become increasingly important to those of us who do not happen to be members of the group to understand its nature and motivation, and one can only understand their motivation if one fully comprehends their culture.

One way to do this is to study 4chan.org. However, the researcher probably will be exposed to heavy loads of trashy pictures and unfunny comments – and the overall picture is difficult to grasp. Another way to study the culture of Anonymous is to read Encyclopedia Dramatica (see Documentation section). On this particular wiki they tell of how they perceive their culture and their reality. Here the researcher can get an overview of their Internet memes, catchphrases, trollings, operations, raids and much more. It is written in their own words, which means that it may

155

be difficult to understand for outsiders due to the groups bizarre in-jokes and esoteric terminology. Personally, it took me a month to grasp of the jargon and to comprehend the basic pictograms of their geek culture. So when I do refer to Encyclopedia Dramatica and Chanarchive it is because I want to document the terminology of 4chan and Anonymous and demonstrate how they think. A researcher must keep in mind that Encyclopedia Dramatica is the public face of 4chan and Anonymous. Encyclopedia Dramatica is of course not the only way to study anonymous. The researcher will have to enter a lot of websites connected to Anonymous besides 4chan, such as Chanarchive, AnonOps, Reddit, Tumblr, YouTube, and many others. In my research the two websites Know Your Meme and Urban Dictionary helped a lot to understand the Internet memes and lingo.

The Internet group Anonymous is a brand new field of research. There isn't a big corpus of literature on this matter. Some studies centers around the dramatic political operations of Anonymous (Sembrat, 2011; Paget, 2012). Other studies are mostly concerned with the anonymity aspect of 4chan and Anonymous (Bernstein et al., 2011; Gekker 2011; Knutilla 2011). Coleman focuses on the historical and cultural aspect of hacking and trolling (Coleman, 2012), while Stryker uses his insights as a long-time user of 4chan to get an understanding of the culture of Anonymous (Stryker, 2011).

As I said, they are, indeed, anonymous which limits the ethnographic study of the group. A researcher cannot approach the group directly on to a single location or even a fixed number of locations, because they are shrouded in secrecy and distributed globally. As the YouTube clip 'Anonymous:Mission' declares:

We are everywhere. We are everyone.

That, however, is not to say they cannot be studied. Anonymous creates countless texts, images, and videos on the Internet. All of these traces of Anonymous activity can be studied as semiotic manifestations of the culture and cultural practices of the internet group. As the researcher learns more and more of these semiotic manifestations from Anonymous websites, the cultural patterns and cultural identity of the group can be implied and understood.

I have personally met with members of the Internet group Anonymous, and I have chatted on the Internet with members that belonged to the group. I could speak with them because I knew and understood their culture. Still, 99% of my knowledge about the group Anonymous comes from analyzing semiotic manifestations on Anonymous related websites rather than from these rare encounters. They mostly confirmed what I already knew. One must remember that the Internet group Anonymous are themselves a product of the semiotic manifestations they produce, consume, and reproduce on the internet.

Trolling

The term 'Internet troll' or 'Internet trolling' refers to the act of luring someone or some people on an Internet forum into becoming aggressive with words – making grammatical errors, using all caps, and writing multiple exclamation marks, sometimes even writing ones instead of exclamation marks due to being upset. The standard trolling method is to enter an Internet forum anonymously, or with a fake identity, and posting a provocative and often ridiculous statement just to see who will take the bait. The victim of such a prank is called a LOLcow; from the abbreviation Laugh Out Loud, combined with the derogatory term cow because they themselves invite trolling (Bishop, 2014). The term has developed following its publication on Encyclopedia Dramatica (see Anex I). The only way to avoid being a LOLcow is not to get into such disputes in the first place. As they say on the Internet (Bins, 2012):

'Don't Feed the Troll!'

4chan became famous for trolling off-guard Internet forums, as those ignorant of the method can't help but become LOLcows. Especially forums with a radical agenda of some kind, whether that would be feminist, ecologist, sport enthusiast, religious, atheist, right wing, left wing etc. are prone to become a target of these pranks. The more hysterical people that attend the forum the easier the prank would be. Later the troll will anonymously show off his trolling accomplishments by uploading the conversation to 4chan as a picture file, and the 4channers will comment on his achievement. The reason behind all of this is to get a laugh at the expense of others; lulz, a term coined by Encyclopedia Dramatica administrator Jameth, a corruption of LOL with much the same conceptual meaning as the German word 'Schadensfreude'. Thus, the common catchphrase used by Internet trolls (Coleman, 2012):

'I did it for the lulz!'

IRL (In Real Life) trolling is different. These are pranks taken into real life situations, that is, practical jokes, often documented on the Internet. IRL trolls are not just harassing Internet forums, but actively encountering the physical public. It must be added that the term IRL is problematic. It is, however, a convenient one, as it has become the common Anonymous term for anything outside the Internet. First of all, a lot of what is called IRL trolling uses media too, but it is 'old media' such as newspapers, telephones, radio and television.

And secondly, the Internet is hardly unreal. Such a separation may work from a naïve perspective, but does not work as a coherent explanation of the Internet. What is done on the Internet may be at a different level of reality, such as, for instance, the rules of a game, but it is not outside reality, and it has real life consequences.

To think of the Internet as outside real lived life is a cyberspace myth that we should try to avoid, because it leads to mistaken perspectives on how the Internet really works (Baym, 2010).

The Case of Mitchell Henderson

On April 20th 2006 a 13 year old Minnesotan boy named Mitchell Henderson, for reasons unknown, shot himself in the head with a .22-caliber rifle he had found in his parents' bedroom. A tragic incident that, had it not been for a MySpace page and a quaint grammatical error, probably wouldn't have gone any further than his next of kin.

Mitchell Henderson was commemorated by friends and family on a MySpace memorial page, in which they expressed their condolences, prayers, and loving memories (Stryker, 2011). One comment from a mourner, though, attracted unplanned popular notice (Stryker, 2011, p.229-30):

> *"He was such an hero, to take it all away. We miss him so, That you should know, And we honor him this day. He was an hero, to take that shot, to leave us all behind. God do we wish we could take it back, And now he's on our minds. Mitchell was an hero, to leave us feeling like this, Our minds are rubber, our joints don't work, Our tears fall into abyss. He was an hero, to take that shot, In life it wasn't his task, He shouldn't have had to go that way, before an decade'd past. Now he sits there in my heart, this hero of mine, Always there to make me smile, Make me feel just fine. He had courage, that boy did, courage in his heart. To take that shot, To end his pain, To tear us all apart. But in the end, he died in courage. Lacking, nevermore, He died a hero, Mitchell did, And we'll love him forevermore. We love you like an brother. We miss you so much. We will always love you, kid. Rest In Peace Mitch. ~Lila"*

Evidently written with the best of intentions, the naively garbled declaration had somewhat strange implications. First of all, it opens up discussion as to what it takes to be a hero. Lila's use of the term "courage" seemed incongruous, given the context. "Courage in his heart" to "tear us all apart"; is that a laudable act of courage? Secondly, the grammatical error of spelling 'an hero' as in 'an hour' appeared peculiar, if not just funny, to people with a dark sense of humor.

The Internet trolling and IRL trolling of Mitchell Henderson´s memorial swiftly took a far more sinister turn. The Henderson family got harassed by some of the anonymous hordes of 4chan. One troll e-mailed Fox 11 News, pretending to be Mitchell Henderson asking advice on how not to lose his iPod. The e-mail was read aloud live by the presenter, who did not know how to react to this pseudoposthumous request with anything apart from weak humor. The video clip documenting the incident, 'Mitchell Henderson E-mails Fox News 11' can be found on YouTube. This kind of trolling is 4chan's way of ridiculing 'old media', unable to keep up with what is going on in the much faster Internet cultures.

The Henderson's got trolled by people one can only assume had connection to 4chan (Schwartz, 2008). They hacked Henderson's MySpace account, giving him the face of a zombie. Someone placed an iPod on Henderson's grave, took a picture and posted it to /b/. Henderson's face was appended to dancing iPods, spinning iPods, hardcore porn scenes. A dramatic re-enactment of Henderson's demise appeared on YouTube, complete with shattered iPod. Mr. and Mrs. Henderson were harrased by phone calls with messages such as 'Hi, this is Mitchell, I'm at the cemetery.' 'Hi, I've got Mitchell's iPod.' 'Hi, I'm Mitchell's ghost, the front door is locked. Can you come down and let me in?'

What was supposed to have been a time of mourning in fact ended up turning into a Henderson nightmare. The trolls of the Internet, due to a minor grammatical error and a misjudgment as regards to glorifying heroes, made their lives a living Hell. While the trolls were doing it for the lulz, the mourning family were the victims of their bizarre kind of amusement.

The Hero

Joseph Campbell's influential hero archetype is defined as a magnification of the formula represented by the rites of passage of separating, initiating and finally returning from the performance of heroic deeds. This formula he names the Monomyth (Campbell, 1993). He explains (Campbell, 1993, p.30):

"A hero ventures forth from the world of common day into a region of supernatural wonder: fabulous forces are there encountered and a decisive victory is won: the hero comes back from this mysterious adventure with the power to bestow boons on his fellow man."

It is obvious, then that the story of Mitchell Henderson does not correspond well with the Monomyth. He may well have ventured forth with his rifle, but shooting oneself is not normally considered a decisive victory, and he did not return with the power to bestow boons on his fellow man-quite the opposite: he deprived his family, not to mention society, of a promising young life. The Monomyth, however, is merely Joseph Campbell's take on the hero archetype. Those historically recognized as heroic may define themselves differently. General Patton addressed the issue of the real hero in his famous speech 'The Invasion of Normandy' in England on May 17th 1944 (Patton, 1974, p.457):

"The real hero is the man who fights even though he's scared. Some get over their fright in a minute, under fire; others take an hour; for some it takes days; but a real man will never let the fear of death overpower his honor, his sense of duty, to his country and to his manhood.

Mitchell Henderson's misfortune fits even worse with the notion of the real hero presented by George Patton. In the case of Mitchell Henderson there is neither honor nor sense of duty to country or manhood: on the contrary, his suicide was an attempt to escape such demands, or, at best, a personal existential choice. Applying the term hero to his act of suicide becomes absurd and involuntarily hilarious, even though the act itself was a serious, tragic event.

Might Mitchell Henderson, then, be considered an anti-hero? Not the opposite of a hero, but a specialized kind of protagonist considered an outlaw or villain by society although the reader or audience identifying with his story sees him as the good guy? (Vogler, 1999). Only if we consider Lila Henderson's "audience". But then again Lila did not say he was a hero, but an hero, and that, it seems, was something else entirely; something to do with killing oneself. An hero, one should then imagine, apparently meant being suicidal.

4chan

The reason Mitchell Henderson and the term an hero has become infamous is due to the Internet imageboard called 4chan (Bergstrom, 2010; Knutilla, 2011) on which anyone can post texts and pictures freely and anonymously. The site is a controversial one that at the time of the events taking place housed the roguish, secret group that would later be known to the public as Anonymous (Paget, 2012).

The 4channers, the cohort of 4chan, posted Lila's words on the 4chan message-board known as Random or /b/, and began to poke fun of it. As the story of an hero spread and multiplied it became an Internet meme. In this process Mitchell Hendersons story turned into an urban legend in which he not only had taken his own life but had done it due to the fact that he lost his iPod (Stryker, 2011). Pure fabrication, but, somehow, it stuck and became a mythical element interlinked with the term 'an hero'.

On 4chan.org the term an hero got its own life on the Internet, so to speak; as this 2007 thread 'truley an hero' from chanarchive.org indicates (see Figure 1).

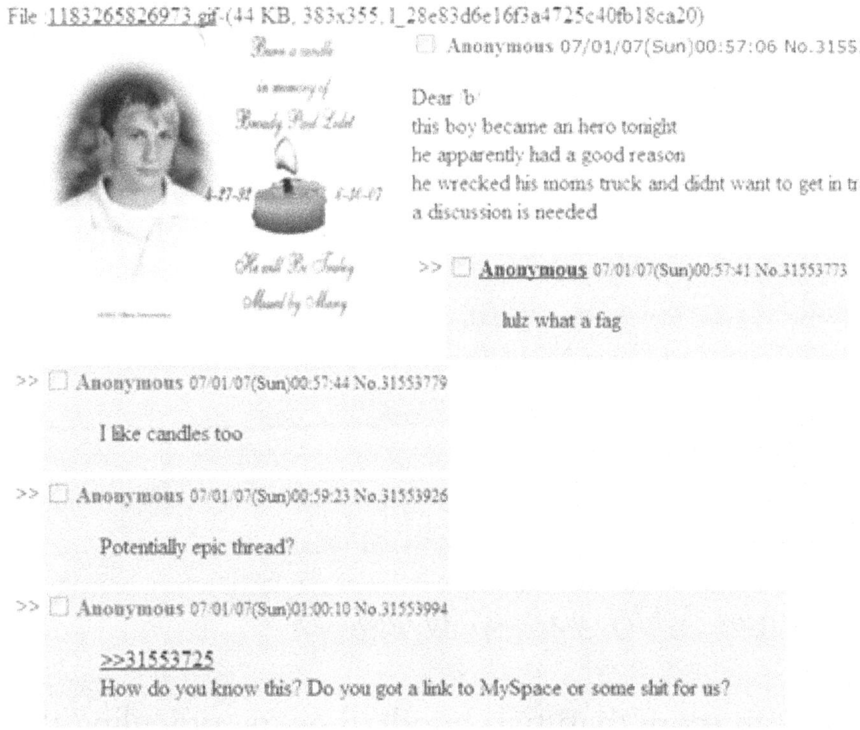

Figure 1: Truley an hero.

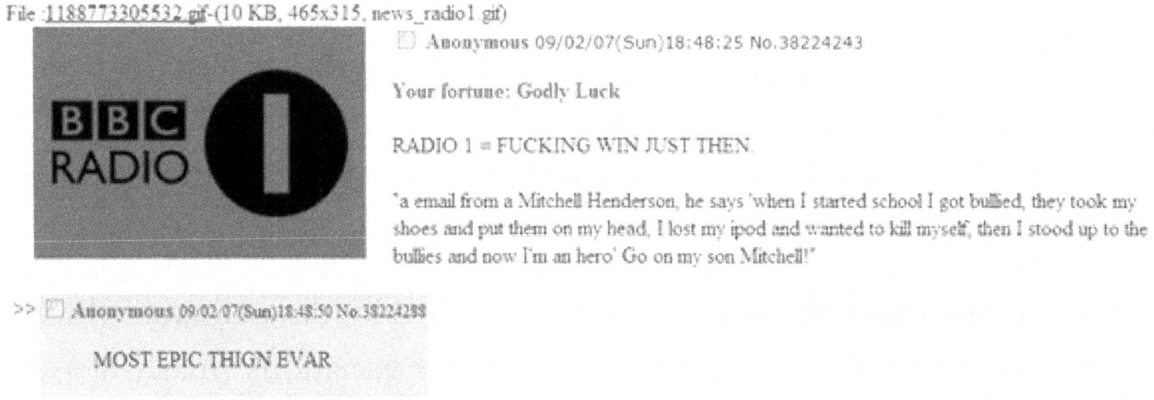

Figure 2. BBC Radio 1 - mudkips on the radio.

Anonymous (ID: UZoSSUYk) 04/09/13(Tue)16:57:19 No.471502624

>>471500235

You nod in acceptance before getting up to leave for your first class. Nothing eventful really happens at least until you get to your fourth period where you meet up with Felicia.

"Hey," she says to you, smiling.

"Hey. I talked to the principal earlier today and I'm going to press charges on him. Should teach that fucker not to play in the moment."

"...Are you really sure that's necessary? I mean I did talk to him earlier and he said he was sorry but he says he still wants me back."

"That's comical, I didn't know a retard could apologize but it doesn't seem like he's going to give you up anytime soon. What's more amusing is that he thinks I'm going to let you down or hurt you, but that won't happen. He started this shit in the first place, so I'm going to finish it like a man with a clear conscience."

With that, the conversation ends and you talk about more lighthearted things until the class ends. You kiss Felicia goodbye and wallow through the rest of the day. On your way to your car you meet up with your sister. She asks how your day was and you fill her in on the events as you drive home to drop her off. You text Felicia asking her if she's available today but you get back a negative answer. That sort of threw out your plans. Do you:

A) Go inside, maybe hang out with your beloved sister.
B) Go into town, find shit to do.
C) Motherfucking an hero.

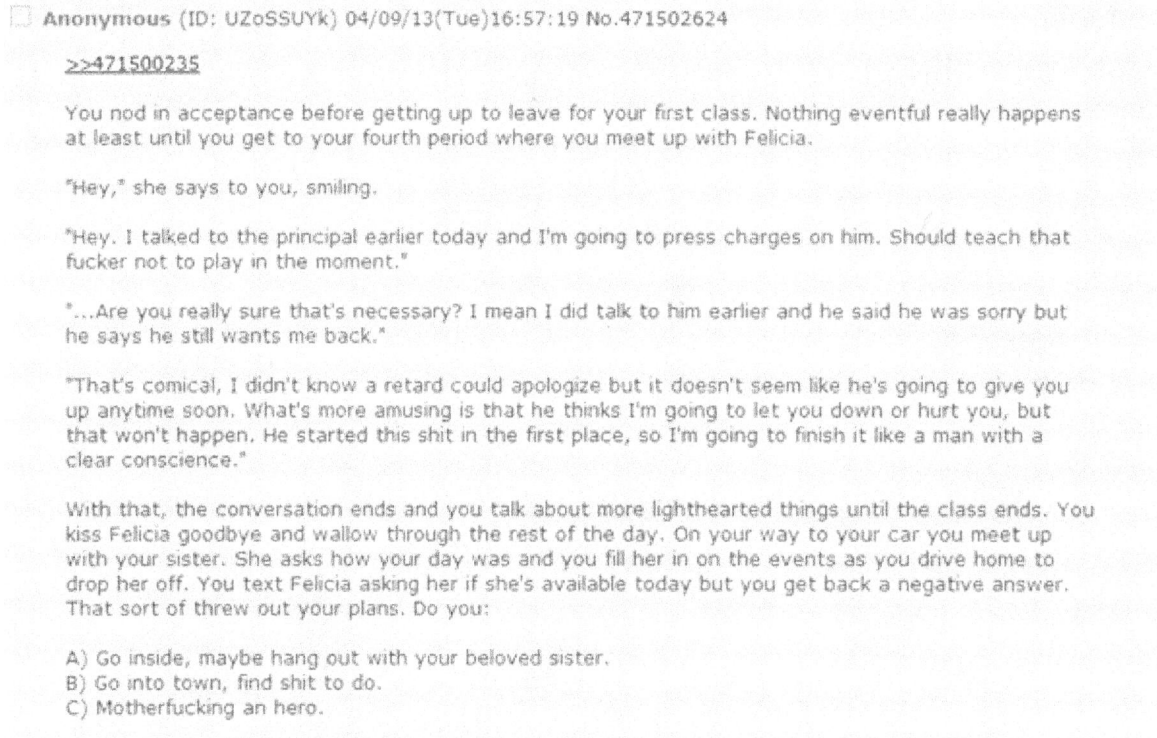

Figure 3. Hey, wake up. (Thread 3).

From here it goes on with more than two hundred posts, ridiculing the boy and his family, but also discussing why a boy would be so afraid of his parents that he would rather shoot himself than face the consequences. The internet meme *an hero* had become well-known among 4channers.

Another Charnarchive example from a 2007 thread "*bbc radio 1 - mudkips on the radio*" involving Mitchell Henderson as "an hero" as can be seen in Figure 2. The Internet meme an hero is still being used on 4chan as the last option in this 2013 Chanarchive thread 'Hey, wake up. (Thread 3)' documents (see Figure 3).

I define an Internet meme as a motif that is virally disseminated through the Internet. The motif often undergoes lots of variations (mash-ups) and may consist of sound, pictures, movie clips, games, and written text, or as is often the case, a combination by two or more modalities. Moreover the motif can be connected to only one of these modalities but need not be and in such case may enter different kinds of modalities.

The term meme is believed to have stemmed from radical skeptic Richard Dawkins. In his use of the term it is considered any cultural idea or behavior, such as fashion, language, religion, science and sports – cultural DNA reproducing itself. It is unclear whether Dawkins memes to be objective structures, or a metaphor for cultural practices. In any case, while the term may historically be traced to Dawkins his influence and thoughts on the matter must be regarded as being of little importance since the term Internet meme has a new colloquial meaning (Davison, 2012). Stryker puts it this way (Stryker, 2011, p.21):

> *"It's difficult to pinpoint a precise time when the word 'meme' started to refer to bits of Internet-borne iconography, like lolcats. I'd guess that Richard Dawkins would scoff at the bastardization of his term, especially since he distanced himself from it before the Internet ever co-opted it. This form of transimission is distinctly different from that of genes. You can't share your genes with your pals."*

Examples of Internet memes may be found at Know Your Meme (knowyourmeme.com). Amongst the most well-known Internet memes are LOLcats, Star Wars Kid, and Epic Fail. Each and every day new memes are spawned and old memes are forgotten. As for the an hero-meme, it became wide spread and still enjoys popularity to this day, even though it is several years old. According to Google Insights for Search it peaked in November 2008 (see Figure 4).

A simple google picture search of the an hero-meme shows pictures combined with texts, such as a skeleton shooting itself in the head with the accompanying text 'AN HERO: You should look into it'; an image of a gun pointing backwards and the text: "AN HERO: Become one"; or a picture of a pale-faced goth painted with crosses beneath the eyes and heavy eyeliner – with the text: *They told me I could become enythingh, [sic!] so I became an hero'*. These pictures are but a few examples from a much larger collection. On YouTube one can find a video clip with the title 'He was an hero' showing senator Robert Budd Dwyer's 1987 suicide, taking a shot to the mouth in front of rolling cameras, accompanied by The Beatles song 'It's been a hard days night'.

During this process the 4channers decided that an hero did not just mean an ordinary suicide, and certainly did not mean hero; it meant a suicide of epic proportions; a suicide to be remembered. Mitchell Henderson's unfortunate fate would certainly not be forgotten. The 4channers merely express their attitudes towards epic suicidal behavior in general. Some of them went as fas as to directly aim their mischief at the mourning Henderson family. They came up with a picture of Mitchell Henderson's teenage, braced face followed by the text: 'FAILURE: Breaking the limits' or 'Get an iPod, they said'. This went as far as to become IRL trolling.

An Hero Day

It did not stop with the harassment of the Henderson family. The term *an hero* had outgrown Mitchell Henderson and become a term in its own right, referring to epic suicides in general. By a freak coincidence, the day that Mitchell Henderson chose to take his own life, April 20th, turned out to be the same date as the Columbine Massacre and Adolf Hitler's birthday. These two events are commemorated on Encyclopedia Dramatica in the 'An hero Day' lookup (see Documentation). Furthermore, Encyclopedia Dramatica notes two suicides the same day in 2007 – the year after Mitchell Henderson's suicide, and an oil rig explosion in the Gulf Coast at the same date, in 2010 (see Figure 5). All of these examples became a part of the an hero mythology the 4channers were constructing, and lead to the notion of a special day to celebrate epic suicides called An hero Day, though it must be noted this day a tasteless in-joke particular to 4chan, rather than something most 4channers would celebrate "IRL".

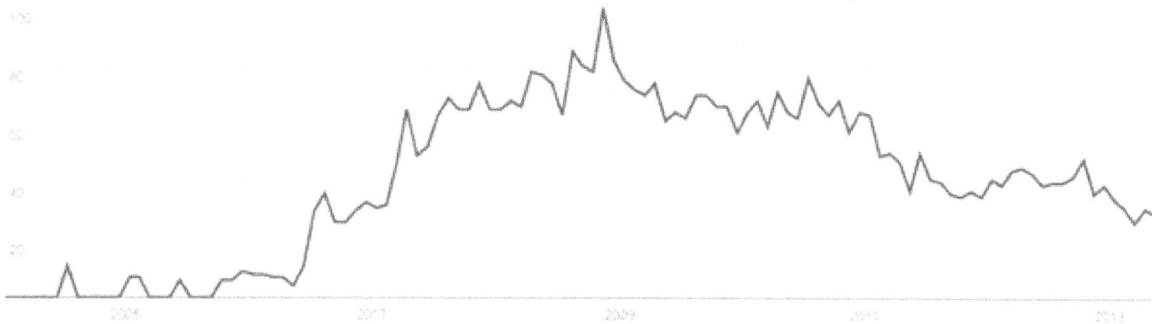

Figure 4. An hero popularity.

An hero Day

- On **April 20, 571** AD, Mohammed was born

- On April 20th, 1889 Adolf Hitler was born. After causing lulz, he became an hero

- On April 20th, 1945 - The US Military captured Leipzig, Germany. Leipzig's mayor killed himself, becoming an hero, but not before he killed his wife and child for the lulz, making him pretty awesome; otherwise nobody would give a shit about him.

- On April 20th, 1999, two kids named Eric and Dylan decided to shoot up their school for the lulz. After killing 13 people, they became an heroes.

- On April 20th, 2006, Mitchell Henderson was having a bad day, and he couldn't find his iPod. He finally couldn't take it anymore, and so he became an hero

- On April 20th, 2007 a man raided mission control ⏍ in Houston and shot a hostage before shooting himself. Houston, we have an hero.

- On April 20th, 2007, Ben Vodden hung himself because his bus driver called him a wank.

- On April 20, 2010, an oil rig off the Gulf Coast called Deepwater Horizon was blown up by muslims. Stoners all over the world didn't notice.

- An hero day is also 4/20, count on many stoners tripping balls as you end yourself

Figure 5. An hero Day.

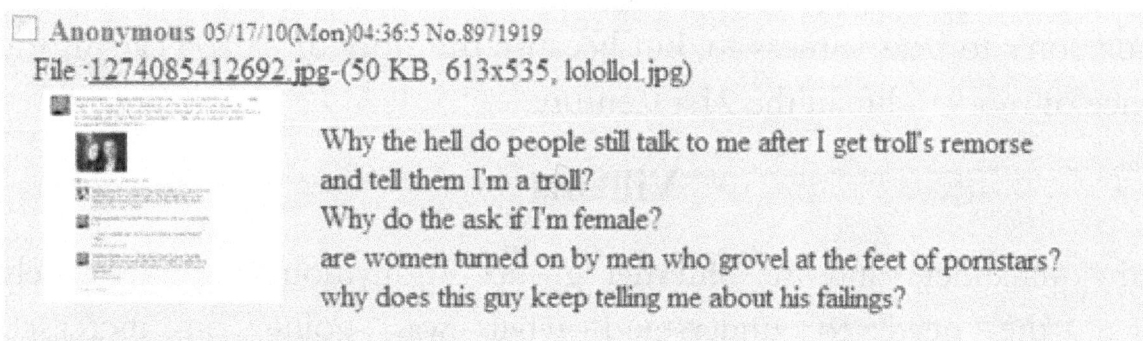

☐ Anonymous 05/17/10(Mon)04:36:5 No.8971919
File :1274085412692.jpg-(50 KB, 613x535, lolollol.jpg)

Why the hell do people still talk to me after I get troll's remorse
and tell them I'm a troll?
Why do the ask if I'm female?
are women turned on by men who grovel at the feet of pornstars?
why does this guy keep telling me about his failings?

Figure 6. Fake Sasha Grey Facebook Trollan.

4channers even suggested that the most epic suicide should be ritually acknowledged each year, and for that reason The Golden iPod Award has, since 2006, been granted unto ill-fated persons that somehow lived up to the 4chan criteria for being an epic suicide, for being an hero. The first to be granted this 'award' was Mitchell Henderson himself, and since then five others have received the dishonor. Encyclopedia Dramatica sums it up in the Golden iPod' article (see Annex I): "The Golden iPod Award is given to one person who managed to become an hero (i.e. commit suicide) in a lulzy way and bring joy to the interwebs. There can only be one Golden iPod each year, and the competition is very tough. The first person ever to receive an Golden iPod was Mitchell Henderson, for his drama-inducing self-pwnage and subsequent posthumous pioneering of the phrase 'an hero'."

While Mitchell Henderson's unfortunate suicide was the starting point, it soon became more. It became a phenomenon. All of the semiological elements, put together in their entirety, point towards something more than the boy who killed himself over an iPod, something more than the travails of his harassed family, and something more than just the lulz. An hero has apotheosized from being an in-joke to becoming, in Roland Barthes terminology, a Myth (Barthes, 1972), thereby showing us some important aspects to our life and death in the Age of the Internet; and how to behave, or, rather, not to behave in social media. It may be considered a Myth not because it did not happen in reality, not because it wasn't hard for the Henderson's to bear witness to, but because the story of *an hero* caught the essence of modern life in the 21st Century.

Villains

As the 4channers and the Internet group Anonymous became widely known, the need to understand what was going on increased correspondingly. One of the first attempts to get a notion of Anonymous outside the group was by Los Angeles Fox affiliate KTTV. On July 26th 2007 The Fox 11 Investigation mentioned, for the first time on main stream media, the existence of Anonymous, referred to as 'hackers on steroids' or 'the Internet hate machine'; the descriptive label 'domestic terrorists' was also used. Hackers on Steroids and The Internet Hate Machine almost immediately became Internet memes, expressing the villainous nature of Anonymous, but, equally, the inanity of Fox television. It is hardly functional to be a hacker on steroids, and the term Internet Hate Machine gives merely some vague impression as to what Anonymous really is; one shrouded in metaphor rather than giving any clear indications of motives and methods; though the trolls recognized the epic quality of such expressions.

In the Fox 11 Investigation feature the Internet group called Anonymous is clearly portrayed as villainous. But what does it mean to be a villain? According to Vogler, inspired by Jungian psychology, we should examine the shadow archetype in order to comprehend this (Vogler, 1999, p.71):

"The negative face of the Shadow in stories is projected onto characters called villains, antagonists, or enemies. Villains and enemies are usually dedicated to death, destruction, or defeat of the hero."

In the case of Mitchell Henderson there really is no hero. Mitchell may be an hero, but as we have analysed he is certainly not a hero; Lila seems forthrightly good-hearted, but no hero; and his family, especially his parents, are clearly the victims. Since there are no heroes, the definition of the villain dissolves into thin air, powerless to eludicate the nature of villains and villainy. The Internet trolls are indeed dedicated to destruction, of sorts, but the definition seems unclear.

What does 'negative face of the Shadow' actually mean? Vogler explains (Vogler, 1999, p.71):

"The archetype known as the 'Shadow' represents the energy of the dark side, the unexpressed, unrealized, or rejected aspects of something. Often it's the home of the suppressed monsters of our inner world. Shadows can be all the things we don't like about ourselves, all the dark secrets we cab't admit, even to ourselves. The qualities we have renounced and tried to root out still lurk within, operating in the Shadow world of the unconscious. The Shadow can also shelter positive qualities that are hiding or that we have rejected for some reason."

The explanation is itself shadowy. What exactly is the 'dark side', 'the unrealized and rejected aspect'? More importantly it adumbrates the obvious fatalities and limitations of such therapeutic approaches. It only relates to the subjective impression of reality, not what is actually going on in the objective world. It may, even, deny the existence of an external, objective reality. Clive Staples Lewis criticizes the Jungian psychology as being a myth that other myths are projected onto, arguing (Lewis, 1966, p.71):

"I am not sure that anyone has satisfactory explained the keen, lasting, and solemn pleasure which such stories can give. Jung, who went furthest, seems to me to produce as his explanation one more myth which affects us in the same way as the rest. Surely the analysis of water should not itself be wet."

What Jungian psychology offers is just such an 'explanation' as that myth tends to give, imparting strong feelings of connections without logical cause and effect: much like astrology or the tarot deck. It works all the time, not because it is actually true but because the mind looks for patterns that fit. Porter (Porter, 2010, p.35) brings forth a more recent definition of villains rather more apt to the Internet trolls: "A constant in the definition of villain is that villains act for themselves and display no remorse over their actions that affect the lives of innocents. They only worry about themselves and remain the most narcissistic or self-involved characters in the story."

170

The Internet trolls did certainly display no remorse over the way in which their actions affected the innocent Henderson family. They seemed only concerned about themselves and their lulz. Actually, Encyclopedia Dramatica refers to a so-called Troll's Remorse in an article of the same name, which they jokingly term a medical condition, to be cured by saying 'I did it for the lulz' three times so not to lose ones hard-earned Internet cred (see Annex I). ED claims that everyone deserves it, so there is no need to feel remorse. Or are they in fact making fun of themselves, their own trollishness? The question of the Troll's Remorse appears to be an ambiguous one.

Troll's Remorse is a catchphrase used on 4chan as a way to display regret, even though it rarely if ever helps the LOLcows or trolling victims (Mitchell, 2012). Here is a comment from 2010 Charnarchive 'Fake Sasha Grey Facebook Trollan', documenting how the phrase Troll's Remorse is used (see Figure 6).

Tricksters and Vigilantes

It would be easy to decry Anonymous as mere villains, were it not for the fact that nowadays Anonymous are recognized, by themselves, at least, as righteous rebels against corrupt governments and immoral corporations. Paget (Paget, 2012, p. 1) states:

"At times citing libertarian ideals (a desire to preserve free enterprise, individual freedoms, freedom of speech, and freedom to circulate information), many activists also argue that the Internet should be free. The Anonymous movement is the epitome of hacktivism. Focusing initially on actions to uphold their notion of the Internet, they have expanded their activities from web actions to struggles that are also happening in the streets."

Hacktivism is a portmanteau of hacking and activism; using computers for political activist purposes (Milan, 2012). Are trolls suddenly hacktivists for a greater cause? On one hand we have a case such as the harassment of the Henderson's, and on the other hand we have the guardians of Internet freedom. How come?

Unsurprisingly, it comes from the multiplicity of factions within 4chan; one including 'oldfags' and 'newfags'. The term fag is derived from the word faggot but has nothing to do with homosexuality, as such. It can be translated as idiot or douche bag. 'Oldfags' and newfags are just different age groups, a conflict between young adults and teenagers. Significantly, we have the '/b/-tards' (rhymes with retards) and the 'moralfags'. These two groups tend towards opposing directions within the Anonymous community. The '/b/-tards' wants to keep on trolling and finding or producing funny images that eventually turn into Internet memes. The 'moralfags' want something more. They want to change the world into a better place for everyone, a world of free speech and information (Stryker, 2011). It seems that they may have split up. The '/b/-tards' have been left behind at 4chan while the 'moralfags' moved on to Reddit, a more political and not quite as chaotic Internet site.

The schism was initiated when Operation Chanology was launched against Scientology in 2008. It became obvious that it was mostly 'moralfags' who wanted to keep on fighting for great justice. Later 'moralfags' have participated in the Green Revolution in Iran, supported WikiLeaks by attacking credit card websites, assisted the North African Spring in 2011, engaged in the Occupy Wall Street protest movement, and fought against political attempts to control the Internet such as ACTA, SOPA and PIPA (Stryker, 2011; Paget, 2012). These are just a few, examples, though the most important ones, of Anonymous political activism during the last four years. It is quite an accomplishment for an Internet group that did not seem to head in that direction at first. So maybe there is more to Anonymous than just pranks. E. Gabriela Coleman (Coleman 2012, p.115) sees them as tricksters:

"If we dare consider these informational pranks in light of the trickster, then perhaps there may be some ethical substance to some, although certainly not all, of their actions."

That may very well be a perspective, although one should be wary of Jungian psychology. As already noted, they see themselves as heroes, although maybe as trickster heroes. They certainly have media power of their own. They can actually speak for themselves.

The YouTube clip, 'Message from Anonymous Protect IP Act', November 16, 2011, provides a useful insight. "The freedom the internet provides has served us well, and driven our intellectual progress, sparked revolutions and changed the lives of many, all of which has been accomplished without the interference of corporations, governments, or any other global institutions until now," they said in the clip. "We must unite and stand up to those who wish to censor the internet. We must protect what is rightfully ours. We must attack in defense of our homeland," they concluded.

By homeland they mean the Internet, one based on the aforementioned false cyberspace myth. In any case, their self-portrayal fits into General George Patton's notion of the hero. They are indeed fighting for what they consider their own country. What is more important, they are fighting for their cultural identity. They stand up to fight against oppression, and in the words of Joseph Campbell they are going into the Internet underground bringing back the boon to fellow man: Internet freedom. Are they then, heroes?

What triggered the 4channers attack on the Henderson family is the fact that they did not know how to behave on the Internet. They did not know the rules, so to speak. They were not cultivated for 21st Century communication; they used the Internet as their personal Diary, not to mention cenotaph. 4chan acted as vigilantes because there were no legitimate means available to adjust the Henderson`s socially; and it got out of hand. Vigilantism is defined as "organized, extralegal movements, the members of which take the law into their own hands" (Brown, 1975, pp.95-6). Vigilantes may see themselves as heroes, but they are out of control and may, in fact, turn out to be more problematic than what they are up against. The problem with Anonymous today is that it is still a vigilante organization.

The case of Mitchell Henderson shows that one should be careful of what ones writes on the Internet. It is a public, global mass media and even though there are lots and lots of information, you will never know for sure who actually reads the message and how they are going to react. Anon warns e-surfers to beware of e-sharks; sometimes by blooding the water.

Discussion

The suicide of Mitchell Henderson, and Lila's commentary on it, gave name to a whole new concept, 'an hero' to describe sensational media suicides. It also tell us that anyone can become infamous on the Internet if they do not know how to behave, if they aren't cultivated to comprehend the dangers of the Internet, and consequently may become victims due to their lack of knowledge on how the Internet works. Furthermore, the Internet group Anonymous has become an example of an ambiguity between villainous and heroic deeds. While they may be the worst of enemies to some innocent people on one hand, they may be friends of Internet freedom, on the other. Anons have become vigilante Internet freedom fighters. But there is a catch. To fight against oppression they have turned towards vigilantism, making their own laws and rules of the Internet, becoming self-proclaimed guardians of the Internet. And as the case of Mitchell Henderson shows, if you by some odd coincidence should not abide to these rules and their laws, Internet Hell may break loose.

To understand Anonymous is not as simple as just reading about their legendary operations. To really get a notion of what is going on it is necessary to examine their distinctive Internet culture. The researcher must excavate deep into the semiotic manifestations of their Internet activity, studying their Internet memes, their trollings, their catchphrases etc. Only by doing this will the research be fruitful in comprehending the reasons behind their actions. This is just a preliminary study of this culture, giving advice on how to approach the Internet group Anonymous, and trying to get a conception of the driving forces and intentions behind the Internet activity of Anonymous. Future studies of Anonymous and their culture is necessary, and although there are obvious limitations with anonymity, following their semiotic manifestations gives the researcher clues as to their cultural deeds.

References

Barthes, R. (1972). Mythologies. London: Paladin.

Baym, N. K. (2010). Personal Connections in the Digital Age. Cambridge/Malden: Polity Press.

Bergstrom, K. (2010). Don't feed the troll": Shutting down debate about community expectations on Reddit.com. First Monday 16 (8).

Bernstein, M. s. et al. (2011). 4chan and /b/: An Analysis of Anonymity and Ephemerality in a Large Online Community. In Proceedings of the Fifth International AAAI Conference on Weblogs and Social Media.

Binns, A. (2012). "Don't Feed the Trolls! Managing Troublemakers in Magazine's Online Communities". Journalism Practice, 6(4) (pp. 547–562).

Bishop, J. (2014). "Representations of 'trolls' in mass media communication: a review of media-texts and moral panics relating to 'internet trolling'." International Journal of Web Based Communities 10 (1)

Brown, R. M. (1975). Strain of Violence: Historical Studies of American Violence and Vigilantism. New York: Oxford University Press.

Campbell, J. (1993). The Hero with a Thousand Faces. London: Fontana Press.

Coleman, E. G. (2012). Phreaks, Hackers, and Trolls: The Politics of Transgression and Spectacle. In M. Mandiberg, The Social Media Reader (pp. 99-119). New York: New York University Press.

Davison, P. (2012). The Language of Internet Memes. In M. Mandiberg, The Social Media Reader (pp. 120-36). New York: New York University Press.

Gekker, A. (2011). Legionnaires of Chaos "Anon" and Governments. In van den Boomen, The Journal of Network Theory: Playground Users in Control, vol. 7, no. 2, April 2011. Utrecht: University of Utrecht, (pp. 38-51).

Knuttila, L. (2011). User unknown: 4chan, anonymity and contingency. First Monday, 16(10).

Lewis, C. S. (1966). On Science Fiction. In W. Hooper, Of Other Worlds: Essays and Stories (pp. 59-73). New York/London: A Harvest Book.

Milan, S. (2012). The Guardians of the Internet? Politics and Ethics of Cyberactivists (and of their Observers). Inter-Asia Roundtable 2012: Methodological and conceptual issues in cyber activism research, 30-31 august.

Mitchell, L. (2012). A Phenomenological Study of Social Media: Boredom and Interest on Facebook, Reddit, and 4chan. Victoria: University of Victoria.

Patton, G. S. (1974). Diary, May 17. In M. Blumenson, The Patton Papers (pp. 456-8). Boston: Da Capo Press.

Paget, F. (2012). Hacktivism: Cyberspace has become the new medium of political Voices. White Paper by McAfee, (pp. 1-34).

Porter, L. (2010). Tarnished Heroes, Charming Villains, and Modern Monsters: Science Fiction in Shades of Gray on 21st Century Television. Jefferson: McFarland & Company, Inc.

Sembrat, E. (2011). Hacktivism: How to Respond and Build Around Hacker Communities. In IS 8300 - Disaster Recovery and Contingency Planning, October 2011.

Stryker, C. (2011). Epic Win for Anonymous: How 4chan's Army Conquered the Web. New York/London: The Overlook Press/Gerald Duckworth Publisher Ltd.

Vogler, C. (1999). The Writer's Journey: Mythic Structure for Storytellers and Screenwriters, 2nd. revised edition. London: Pan Books.

Documentation

Anonymous Central. (2011, November 16). Dear citizens of the internet. http://anoncentral.tumblr.com/post/12930371338/dear-citizens-of-the-internet-citizens-of-free.

anonymous1996x. (2012, March 20). Anonymous:Mission.

http://www.youtube.com/watch?v=o1d6dEzYDOc.

Chanarchive. (2007, September 2). bbc radio 1 - mudkips on the radio.

http://chanarchive.org/4chan/b/1384/bbc-radio-1-mudkips-on-the-radio.

Chanarchive. (2013, April 9). Hey, wake up. (Thread 3).

http://chanarchive.org/4chan/b/68737/hey-wake-up-thread-3.

Chanarchive. (2010, May 17). Fake Sasha Grey Facebook Trollan.

http://chanarchive.org/4chan/r9k/5774/fake-sasha-grey-facebook-trollan.

Chanarchive. (2007, July 1). truley an hero.

http://chanarchive.org/4chan/b/298/truley-an-hero.

Encyclopedia Dramatica. (2013, April 25). An Hero Day.
http://encyclopediadramatica.se/An_hero#An_hero_Day.

Encyclopedia Dramatica. (2013, April 25). Golden iPod.
http://encyclopediadramatica.se/Golden_iPod.

Encyclopedia Dramatica. (2013, April 25). Lol-cow.

https://encyclopediadramatica.se/Lol-cow.

Encyclopedia Dramatica. (2013, April 25). Troll's Remorse.
http://encyclopediadramatica.se/Troll's_Remorse.

Schwartz, M. (2008, August 3). The Trolls Among Us. New York Times.

Section 3: Society and Politics

Social Media and the Freedom of Expression in Nigeria: Posting the mind of a Nation

Joseph Wilson and Nuhu Gapsiso

Abstract: Nigerians cherish the freedom they are guaranteed under the United Nations Declaration of Human Rights and other international human rights Instruments and the constitution especially section 39(1) of the 1999 constitution of Nigeria which guarantees freedom of expression as a fundamental right. But the collective commitment to freedom of expression in Nigeria is often tested when these expressions are conveyed via popular conventional channels. Nigerians rights to free expression has over the years been characterised by numerous attempts by state and non-state actors to suppress or bully them into silence. However, the emergence of social media platform and the overwhelming embrace by Nigerians have changed the status quo, as more Nigerians take to social media to express their views on all issues and the perceived use by political and other elites to reach out to supporters. For example the incumbent President of Nigeria has from time to time used his Facebook platform to address Nigerians on some important government decisions and policies that elicits response from Nigerians via same platform. Media organizations have also used the same platform to generate comments on some issues of national interest (e.g. Removal of fuel subsidy, corruption in Nigeria etc.). This paper explores people´s posts on the Facebook site of selected media organizations on the popular Nigeria´s aviation ministry armoured car scandal. The analysis would look at the tone of the posts (positive or negative, sectional based on regional and ethnic affiliation) and the overriding position.

Keywords: Social media, Freedom of Expression, Facebook, Nigeria

Introduction

Nigerians are passionate about expressing their minds on issues of national importance. These expressions cut across all spheres of national endeavours- politics, religion, family, economy, culture, corruption, government policies, sports etc. and the media serve as channels. The social media platform has emerged in recent years to be widely explored and utilized by Nigerians to post comments that, to a large extent represent the opinions of many Nigerians. Conventional Media organizations in Nigeria and diaspora have cashed-in on the popularity of these social media by sharing news stories on their social media accounts, which often times attract speedy comments from Nigerians. However, these comments are often not devoid of showcasing Nigeria´s diversity in terms of ethnicity, religion, political ideology etc. They could sometimes be offensive in nature. This paper explores people´s comments on the Facebook accounts of two popular media organizations (Premium Times and Sahara Reporters) on national issues that have attracted a lot of comments from Nigerians. The Nigeria´s Ministry of Aviation armoured car scandal has continued to attract comments from Nigerians. The paper looks at the tone of the comments (positive or negative, sectional based on regional and ethnic affiliation) and the popular position.

Freedom of expression is an important component of national and individual development.it is a key to dignity and fulfilment at both nation and individual levels. Free expression enables individual to gain an understanding of his surroundings and the wider world by exchanging ideas and information freely with others. It also influences and promotes positively, good governance by enabling citizens to voice their concerns and opinions on issues of probity and accountability with the Authorities. If people can express their views without intimidation and the media are allowed to report what is being said, the government can be kept abreast of people´s concerns and address them (article19.org, 2014). It is therefore not surprising that people worldwide uphold the freedom they are guaranteed under the United Nations Declaration of Human Rights and other international human rights Instruments. Unfortunately, the collective commitment to freedom of expression globally is often tested when state or non-state actors suppress these expressions conveyed via popular conventional channels such as newspapers, television directly or indirectly.

Interestingly, the emergence of social media platform especially, Facebook and twitter etc. has transformed the exercise of freedom of expression especially in societies like Nigeria where significant constraints over traditional media and participation still exist. Individuals now have the opportunity to freely express their minds on any issue of human interest and most interesting is citizen's ability to use the social media to express their positions on issues of national interest.

Social Media

Social media web- based and mobile technologies used for interactive communication Social media comprise the Internet and mobile phone based tools for sharing and discussing information. It is a blend of computing, telecommunications, and interactivity through a platform to communicate via words, videos, audio and visual (Paranjoy, 2012). Social media also refers to web or mobile-based platform that enables an individual or agency to communicate interactively and enables exchange of user generated content (Tiwari and Gosh, 2013). Kaplan and Haenlein (2010) see social media as internet-based application that centres on the web 2.0 (interactive platform) technological ideology that allows the creation and exchange of user-generated content.

Types of Social Media

There are several classifications of the social media with overlaps among various services. One social media service can carry features of another service. For instance, Facebook has micro blogging features with their 'status update'. Also, Flickr and YouTube have comment systems similar to that of blogs (Grahl, 2014). Grahl (2014) notes that as you think through all the options for engaging social media, they all fall into 6 broad categories (social network, book marking sites, social news, media sharing, micro bogging, blog comments and forums). Similarly, Kaplan and Haenlein (2010) outlined 8 broad categories of Social Media. They include:

Social networks

Social networks are online services that enables users connect with other people of similar interest or background. It involves creating virtual networks by likeminded people. It proffers facilities such as chat, instant messaging, photo sharing, video sharing, updates etc. For example Facebook and LinkedIn.

Blog

Blog is a shared online journal where individuals or a group post diary entries about their experiences, opinions, hobbies and may contain text, photos and links to other websites. Blog ordinarily are interactive in nature, which enables of readers to leave comments and the comment trail can be followed.

Micro blogs

Micro blogs are similar to blogs. However, micro blogs focus on short updates that are sent to subscribers. For example twitter (is a micro blogging site that enables its users to send and read 'tweets'). Micro blogs are typically restricted of 140 characters or less.

Wikis

Wiki is a collaborative website service that allows multiple users to create and update pages on particular or interlinked subjects. These multiple pages are linked through hyperlinks and allow users to interact in a complex and non- linear manner. A single page is referred to as 'wiki page'; the entire related content on that topic is called a 'Wiki'. The most popular is Wikipedia, but other examples include Library Blog Wikis, Charles Sturt Library Wiki, Tolkien Wiki, among others.

Vlogs and Video Sharing sites

Video blogs (Vlogs) are blogging sites that primarily use video as the major form of content and in some cases supported by text. For example you Tube. It is one of the most popular video sharing sites. It is a video live casting and video sharing site where users can upload, share, view videos and leave comments.

Social Bookmarking

These services allow users to save, organize and manage links to various websites and Internet resources. Links are tagged (labelled) to allow for easy search and sharing .The most popular are Stumble Upon and Delicious.

Social News

These services allow users to post various news items or links to outside articles and allow them to vote and comment on the items. Voting is the major social aspect, as the items that get the most votes are displayed as the most prominent. Popular examples of Social News are Digg, Propeller and Reddit.

Media Sharing

These services allow users to upload and share various media such as photos or videos. Users also have the opportunity of commenting on the shared media. The most popular are Flickr and YouTube.

Freedom of Expression

The concept freedom of expression dates back to ancient times of the Greek Athenian era more than 2400 years. The widely used international definitions of freedom of expression is provided in article 19 of The Universal Declaration on Human Rights (UDHR) and the International Covenant on Civil and Political Rights (ICCPR), summarised as the freedom to freely express ones opinion without interference:

"Everyone has the right to freedom of opinion and expression; this right includes freedom to hold opinions without interference and to seek, receive and impart information and ideas through any media and regardless of frontiers." (Article 19, Universal Declaration of Human Rights, 1948 (UDHR))

"Everyone shall have the right to hold opinions without interference. Everyone shall have the right to freedom of expression; this right shall include freedom to seek, receive and impart information and ideas of all kinds, regardless of frontiers, either orally, in writing or in print, in the form of art, or through any other media of his choice." (Article 19 (2), International Covenant on Civil and Political Rights, 1966 (ICCPR))

Freedom of expression is not only important in its own right but is also essential if other human rights are to be achieved .It is globally seen as underpinning human rights and democratic freedoms in that it guarantees the exchange of views and opinions necessary to inform and stimulate public debate as well as supporting freedom of association, the questioning

186

and challenging of public officials etc. It has long been valued as a foundation right in all democratic societies (Puddephatt and Oesterlund, 2012). At an individual and national levels, freedom of expression is key to the development, dignity and fulfilment of every person wishes and for good government and therefore for economic and social progress respectively.

Freedom of speech and expression centres on the notion that people have the right to freely express themselves through any media and frontier without interference, such as censorship, and without fear of reprisal or molestation, threats and persecutions. However, it is important to note that, freedom of expression is not absolute, as it carries with it special duties and responsibilities therefore it may be subject to certain restrictions provided by law (Tiwari and Gosh, 2013).

In the same vein Nigeria like any nation of the world is guaranteed freedom expression under its constitution especially Chapter 4 section 39 (1) of the 1999 constitution of Nigeria, which guarantees freedom of expression as a fundamental right. It states that:

39(1) Every person shall be entitles to freedom of expression, including freedom to hold and to receive and impart ideas and information without interference.

This can only be achieved through access to accurate, fair and unbiased information, representing a plurality of opinions, and the means to actively communicate vertically and horizontally, thereby participating in the active life of the community (Wakawa, 2013). But the collective commitment to freedom of expression in Nigeria is often tested when these expressions are conveyed via popular conventional channels. Nigerians rights to free expression has over the years been characterised by numerous attempts by state and non-state actors to suppress or intimidate Nigerians into silence. However, the emergence of social media platform and the overwhelming embrace by Nigerians have changed the status quo, as more Nigerians take to social media to post their views on all issues and its use by politicians and other elites to reach out to supporters. Nigerians, do not hesitate in taking to social media to "dish out" opinions on any issue. Nigerians embrace of the social media is so profound that even public officials as high as the President and members of his cabinet and State Governors all have viable social media accounts especially Facebook which they use periodically to comment on issues of national importance.

As Nigerians explore this new found "citizen-social media romance as means of expressing their views on issues that concerns the nation, these expressions are often characterised by the diversity of a nation in terms of religion, political interest, ethnic and regional affiliations etc. These comments are sometimes offensive.

Freedom of Expression and Social Media in Nigeria

According to Erjavec and Kovačič (2013), an important turning point in the history of audience participation in news is connected to the development of new technologies. Chung (2007) notes that with the use of the internet and its components such as the social media participatory journalism has changed from the top-down journalistic model to a bottom-up phenomenon of information distribution, with the news audience having the possibility of increased control over, and greater involvement in, the news consumption process. The development of new media technology has meant a change from the old way of writing letters to editors: the editorial staffs are more accessible and the former barriers of time and space are considerably lower with new technology (Bergström, 2008).

Audience are now able to instantly interact with traditional content providers through interactive facilities such as comments on news sites and social media (Bergström, 2008)

The Social Media has become a vital communication tool through which individuals can exercise their rights to freedom of expression and exchange information and ideas. In recent times the greater number of individuals and groups have taken to the social media to mobilize support and challenge inequality, corruption and advocate for change in government policies and accountability. The social media has often played an important role in this regard (OHCHR, p.201). In such movements, the Internet and Social Media has often played a key role by enabling people to connect and exchange information instantly and by creating a sense of solidarity. Recent examples include: the Arab Spring that changed the history of the North African countries of Egypt. Tunisia and Libya

In Nigeria, Occupy Nigeria was a socio-political protest movement that began in Nigeria on Monday, 2 January 2012 in response to the fuel subsidy removal by the Federal Government of President Goodluck Jonathan on Sunday, 1 January 2012. Protests took place across the country and at the Nigerian High Commission in London. At least the use of social media services such as Twitter and Facebook was a prominent feature of the protest. Facebook group pages were created to spur Nigerians globally against the fuel-subsidy removal regime. An example is "Nationwide Anti-Fuel Subsidy Removal: Strategies & Protests" which was created on 2 January 2012 had over 20,000 members by 9 January 2012. Student websites in universities and blogs were used to report the Occupy Nigeria protests. Twitter was also extensively used as a connecting platform for the protesters across the nation.

The scenario was different before the emergence of the Internet and the social media as a platform for citizen engagement in freely expressing their various opinions on national issues. Nigeria spends greater part of its existence since independence under military rule, which spanned 30 years. Between 1966–1979 and 1983– May1999, there were several decrees and laws that infringed upon the rights of Nigerians including their freedom of expression. The media being the major channels of expression for Nigerians were restricted in various ways especially access, ownership control and manipulation. Not a few journalists and citizens have suffered humiliations, threats, arrests and even untimely deaths in the hands of politicians and law enforcement agencies over reports, opinion and expressions the authorities and highly placed individuals found unpleasant even when such views are correct (Akingbolu, 2013).

In recent times, governments across the globe have tried to withhold information from the common man under one pretext or another. But, with the advent of social media vested with the immense power of delivering information to the masses and enabling them to make comments and share opinion against or for such information. Although attempts were made by Governments to carefully regulate Internet, its impact on information sharing is still unimaginable high compared to conventional media platform (Television, Newspapers etc.). Facebook has for a long time been a popular destination for Nigerians online with many Nigerians setting up their first Internet accounts on the platform. The number of Nigerians that have signed up to Facebook, as a means of communication and interactions, has continued to increase over the years.

For example from 400, 000 between 2008 and 2010 to 4.3 million mark at the end of December 2011 (Elebeke, 2012). In 2012 Nigeria became Africa's second largest country on Facebook, after Egypt with over 6 million users (TechLoy, 2012). It was reported in 2013 that Nigeria has overtaken South Africa to become Facebook's largest user base in Sub Saharan Africa with over 11 million users (CP-Africa.com, 2013). With this enormous number of users, it is obvious that there is hardly a moment of each day that you don't find Nigerian Facebook users Online. Their online presence on Facebook is often characterised by several activities such as, chat, discussion, comments, visual/audio uploads, updates about daily routine of subscribers, news update from various organizations etc. It is a handy platform for quickly measuring opinions of millions of Nigerian users on several personal, national and international issues, which usually cuts across all subject (sports, family, crime, education, corruption etc.). For example corruption allegations against government officials always attract huge discourse among Nigerians. This paper centres on one of such issues.

Facebook and Nigeria's Minister of Aviation Armoured BMW Car Scandal

Recently Nigerians took to Facebook to freely express their views on national issues that centred on the Nigeria´s Ministry of Aviation officials over an inflated price of two BMW armoured cars. Popularly referred to by most media organizations as "Nigeria's Minister of Aviation Armoured BMW Car Scandal "generated a lot of comments from Nigerians.

On 16 October 2013 a web-based News media (Sahara Reporters) reported that:

> *a cash-strapped agency of the Ministry of Aviation purchased two armoured BMW 760 Li cars for the private use of Aviation Minister Stella Oduah, several automobile sales companies have indicated that the cars were massively overpriced.*

Our report yesterday disclosed that the Nigerian Civil Aviation Authority (NCAA) paid:

> *"approximately $1.6 million to buy the two cars from Coscharis Motors Limited in Lagos, meaning that each car cost close to $800,000. But our investigations with car sale companies revealed that the NCAA could have got eight, not two, BMW armoured cars for their money........at each of the BMW cars could have been provided to the NCAA for $200,000 plus the cost of shipping to Nigeria (Sahara Reporters, 2013)*

Premium Times, another popular web based newspaper reported the story and gave updates on the report. Most recent was its headline:

BREAKING: Jonathan drops corrupt Aviation Minister, Stella Oduah, 3 others.

President Goodluck Jonathan has accepted the resignation of four cabinet ministers.

They are Minister of Aviation, Stella Oduah; Minister of Police Affairs, Caleb Olubolade; Minister of Niger Delta Affairs, Godsday Orubebe; and Minister of State for Finance, Yerima Ngama.

They were asked to resign to save them the humiliation of being sacked. It is not immediately clear why Messrs Olubolade, Orubebe and Ngama were asked to leave. But Mrs Oduah was sent packing over corruption-related offences. Both the House of Representatives and a presidential committee for compelling an agency under her supervision, the Nigerian Civil Aviation Authority, NCAA, to buy her two exotic armoured cars in violation of Nigeria's public procurement laws, indicted her (Premium Times, 2014).

These and other related reports were also shared on the Facebook accounts of the two popular online news media and afforded Nigerians the opportunity to freely express their positions on the issue. What are the discourse characteristics of these comments on the Facebook sites of the two news media (Sahara Reporters and Premium Times)? Are the comments positive (in favour of the Minister) or negative (against the Minister), sectional based on regional and ethnic affiliation (are the comment based on her ethnic and regional affiliation? What is the overriding position (More in favour or more against the Minister) Are there offensive or abusive comments?

Method

Critical Discourse Analysis (CDA) and Discursive Psychology approaches were used to address the research questions. Critical discourse analysis provides theories and methods for the empirical study of the relations between discourse and sociocultural developments in various social domains (Jorgensen and Phillips, 2002). Discourse analysis is a useful method for uncovering discrimination or nature of discourses in news items (Van Dijk, 1988; Richardson, 2007). Critical discourse analysis is an interdisciplinary approach to the study of discourse that views language as a form of social practice and focuses on the ways social and political domination are reproduced in text and talk (Norman and Holes, 1995). CDA does not limit its analysis to specific structures of text or talk, but systematically relates these to structures of the socio-political context. The aim of critical discourse analysis is to shed light on the linguistic discursive dimension of social and cultural phenomena and processes of change in late modernity. It is also designed to contribute to social change along the lines of more equal power relations in communication processes and society in general.

According to Jorgensen and Phillips (2002), Discursive Psychology centres on language use in everyday text and talk – is a dynamic form of social practice, which constructs the social world, individual selves and identity. Discursive psychology deploys many of the same methods as other qualitative approaches. As in other qualitative approaches, research questions in discursive psychology point in the direction of analyses of the production of meaning. But discursive psychology differs from other qualitative approaches in being interested in how meanings are produced within the discourses or repertoires that people draw on as resources in order to talk about aspects of the world (Jorgensen and Phillips, 2002). Discursive Psychology deploys many of the same methods (coding, transcription, interview etc.) as other qualitative approaches.

Procedure

Two news media were purposively selected for this study. The choice of the two news media was purposive because they first broke the news on the armoured car and followed and gave an update on the scandal to the point of the Minister´s resignation. They are also news media that have a large followership among Nigerian due to their investigative journalism qualities and proactive posture against corruption in governance and also coverage of issues of national importance that often times are overlooked by conventional news media organizations especially in Nigeria.

Sahara Reporters is a Nigeria online news media in the diaspora while Premium Times is a home-based online newspaper. To effectively analyse the discourse, reader's comments under the news item posted on Facebook walls of the selected online news media, themes were drawn based on the objectives of the study. Comments posted on the walls of the two news media were read and reread in order to identify and place them in the relevant themes or categories. The themes included: comments considered to be offensive, abusive, comment with ethnic or regionally inclination, comments that are positive and negative. Comments that attacked the dignity of the subject, comments based on the political orientation or affiliation of the subject and comments that centred on the news media instead of the subject.

To identify the key messages in comments, which included offensive speech, we conducted an analysis of macro propositions. According to Van Dijk (1980), macro propositions analysis is based on an identification of the most relevant collection of information in a text, derived from the local meanings of words and sentences by macro rules, such as deletion, generalisation and construction. Such rules combine similar meanings with construct different meaning constituents in higher-level events or social concepts, which enable one to identify the main idea news item or even multiple news items or comments. The study also included an analysis of keywords, which constituted a particular discourse. Keywords direct discursive attention towards a specific segment of the society (Fowler, 1991). In this case the study looked at the comments that tilted towards to regional or ethnic affiliation, political affiliation and orientation. The findings were quantitatively and qualitatively presented.

Results

A total of 250 comments were identified and analysed based on the various themes. The positive comments were negligible when compared to the negative comments. From the 250 comments analysed only 23 were in favour of the Minister. Some of the examples are:

"Stella actually made a great difference in Aviation, she was a hardworking minister. She did well in the face lift of Airport facilities across the country"

"Aviation Minister So Far....your criticisms will not change that fact....he without sin should cast the first stone"

"PRINCESS STELLA ODUAH the great daughter of NDI IGBO, your good works and excellent performances in the time u spent as aviation minister speaks for itself, u are the best aviation minister so far, history will judge......."

"As a matter of d records Adewumi Adesina & Stella r d best minister prior to her sack in dis country we sacrifise excellence on d alter of personal interest"

The negative comments were overwhelming. Out of the 250 comments analysed from both news media only 23 where in favour of the minister. 227 comments were not in favour of the minister. The negative comments were a combination of attack on her personality, abusive and offensive. Some of the abusive or negative comments were even extended to her political affiliation and the President of the country. Examples of such comments include:

"shameless criminal woman"

"She Must be Persecuted by d Laws of Nigeria, otherwise, all Robbers in jails Deserve Freedom 2!"

"yeah i agree with u she is the best aviator and the best thief"

"You don't fire thieves, you jail them."

"Oduah has ruined her own career in Nigeria polity. Corrupt female minister for that matter."

"Mrs BMW."

"Finally,the chiken(thief)has come home 2 roast"

Some of the comments were tilted towards regional and ethnic affiliation. Some of the comment were in favour of the minister and praised her for being a worthy ambassador of her kinsmen. While some saw her action as an embarrassment to her ethnic group (Igbo people).Some of the crucial macro propositions were the following:

"u pple shul live that woman alone, the car belong to ministry and not her, those enemy of progress that call for her sack is becos she has build international airport in igbo land that diverted igbo businessmen to igboland.."

"Anti-North Minister is Out."

"Are those cars registered in her name? Why the noise? Is it because she gave the igbos what Nigeria thought the igbos will never get"

"Ojoro, we the igbos are proud of her"

"I don't even know why all these igbos ar supporting this woman, anyway, they ar all d same......greedy people"

"PRINCESS STELLA ODUAH the great daughter of NDI IGBO, your good works and excellent performances in the time u spent as aviation

minister speaks for itself, u are the best aviation minister so far, history will judge"

"How abt d stolen money or must we be quite bcz she z so called thief ndi igbo?"

"am so ashame of some comments by some of my Igbo brothers.must ethnicity n tribal colouration be introduced in every discussion?...udua 's action must be condemned by any sane person"

These comments either tried to portray the minister as a worthy ambassador of the Igbo people, who are one of the major ethnic groups in Nigeria living in the South East of Nigeria. However, some of the comments also criticised the ethnic group for producing a leader that has brought shame to her kinsmen. Others focussed on the issue rather than the ethnic or regional background of the Minister. They condemned the action of the minister.

Our critical discourse analysis showed that writers made different kinds of offensive and abusive comments. A notable common feature was that writers criticise the personality involved and also attacked the news media . Some few selected comments are as follows:

"Is she married mi I want to marry her as second wife so that we enjoy BMWssss"

"shameless criminal woman"

"Cary go,olee (Thief)"

"USELESS SAHARA REPORTER....."

The analysis revealed that there were comments that attacked the personality of the minister mostly labelling her as "thief". Some of the posts or comments include:

"Thieves ole carry am go"

"oh GOD save our country from the evil and useless leaders"

"shameless criminal woman"

"Ashawo (prostitute) dis is jst b4 u go to hell fire if u die as u r now"

"she's Jezebel witch.....bitch minister"

"A rogue is a rogue; can she spend her stolen loots on those cars???"God is watching".

The attack on her personality focused on her being dishonest and the act was unlawful

"This woman is just a common criminal"

There were also comments that touched on her political affiliation. The minister belonged to the People Democratic Party (the ruling party in Nigeria). The comments generalised attack on the Ministers political affiliation. One of the comments was calling for protection against the main opposition party (All People's Congress): Some examples are:

"She should be protected against apc and boko haram"

"Stella Oduah is a certified pen-robber, working in tandem with Jonathan led PDP anti-masses and most corrupt-ridden government in Nigeria history"

Some of the comments were direct attack on the news media organization for being biased and over blotting the issue and overlooking other public office holders who have don worst. They tried to discredit journalists by presenting them as biased because of their dislike of the minister. However some of the comments commended the effort of the news media for fighting corruption. Some examples are:

"At the end of the day the devil premium times and Sahara reporters will be disappointed. Ganging up against our dear princess will never succeed"

"its not news again, hip hip Sahara Reporter,dont fool ur self, why not we report the good side of that woman also."

"Is obviously that there's an issue between sahara Report and stella Odoah when it comes to her issue of report"

"USELESS SAHARA REPORTER....."

The overriding position was the negative or comment not in favour of the minister. A total 250 comments from the two news media were analysed out of which only 23 where in favour of the minister. The other 227 comments were against the minister's action a number of which were abusive.

Discussion

Conventional journalism mostly enabled audience participation through letters to editors or writing complaints, which journalists either took into consideration for future reference, or immediately published as corrections. But the major challenge with this form of audience participation in journalism process is that it does not guarantee the publishing or broadcast of such contributions. This obviously hinders freedom of expression. It is often the case that comments, articles, opinion from audience that does not meet the interest of media owners, relations and friend of media owners are often left unpublished, whether the opinion is in the interest of the nation. This is not the case at the moment, as the emergence of the Internet has greatly enhanced audience participation or engagement in news process. Audience now have the opportunity of posting comments under news items with little or no hindrance. The social media have emerged to be a viable tool for realising freedom expression as people take to social media of their choices to express their opinions freely on any issue. There is the major challenge of abusing the opportunity of participatory online journalism by using offensive speech (Karlsson, 2008).

Nigerians prolonged military rule and the problem of poor access to conventional media has for several years deprived them of freely expressing themselves on important issues. The Social media now gives them the opportunity to freely express their views on any issue and as it pleases them. The Minister of Aviation BMW car scandal has shown that Nigerians are waiting for any breaking news to take to social media accounts to express their minds.

The main finding from the critical discourse analysis was that comments included more negative comments (against the action of the Minister) than positive comment (in favour of the minister). There were also comments that were general attacks on human dignity, attacks based on supposed political affiliation, attacks based on supposed regional and ethnic affiliation. There were also attacks on the news media organization.

The conclusion of this study is that the social media platform has actually improved Nigerians rights to free expression. However, there is a clear abuse of the idea of participatory journalism. According to Erjavec and Kovačič (2013), "with the excuse of audience participation, personal attacks on personalities in comments under news items are tolerated. According to Tiwari and Gosh (2013), it is clearly evident that social media is a very powerful means of exercising one's freedom of speech and expression. However, increasing abuse has given force to the Government's attempts at censoring social media. What is therefore desirable is regulation of social media through a specific legislation not its censorships. While Nigerians post their minds, some level of decency is required and issues should be addressed rather than personality.

References

Bergström, A. (2008) "The Reluctant Audience: Online Participation in the Swedish Journalistic Context", Westminster Papers in Communication and Culture, 5 (2): 60–80.

Chung, D. S. (2007) "Profits and Perils: Online News Producers' Perceptions of Interactivity and Uses of Interactive Features", Convergence: The Journal of Research into New Media Technologies, 13 (1), 43–61.

Erjavec, K. and Kovačič M.P (2013) Abuse of Online Participatory Journalism in Slovenia: Offensive Comments under News Items. Medij. istraž. 19, (2) ,55-73

Federal Government of Nigeria (1999) Constitution of Nigeria, Abuja, Federal Government of Nigeria

Fowler, R. (1991) Language in the News. London, New York: Routledge.

Jorgensen, M and Phillips, L. (2002) Discourse analysis as theory and method. London, SAGE Publications

Kaplan A. M. & Haenlein M. (2010), Users of the World, Unite! The Challenges and Opportunities of Social Media, Business Horizons, vol. 53, 2010, pp. 59-68

Karlsson, M. (2008) Increasingly interactive: Swedish online news 2005–2007. Montreal, Quebec: International Communication Association

Norman, F. and Holes, C (1995). Critical Discourse Analysis: The Critical Study of Language. Longman

Paranjoy G. T. (2012) Media Ethics (New Delhi: Oxford University Press, p. 354.

Puddephatt, A. and Oesterlund P. (2012) Freedom of expression, media and digital communications, Berlin, The European Commission

Richardson, J. E. (2007) Analysing Newspapers. New York: Palgrave Macmillan.

Van Dijk, T. A. (1980) Macrostructures. Hillsdale: Lawrence Erlbaum

Documentation

Akingbolu R.(19 May, 2013) World Press Freedom Day: How Free is the Nigerian Press?, ThisDay Newspaper. Retreived 8/2/2014 from http://www.thisdaylive.com/articles/world-press-freedom-day-how-free-is-the-nigerian-press-/147821/

Article 19.org, (2014) Freedom of expression. What we do. article19.org. Retrieved 8/2/2014 from http://www.article19.org/pages/en/freedom-of-expression.html

CP-AFRICA.COM (2013) Over 11 million Nigerians on Facebook; becomes Facebook's largest user base in Sub Saharan Africa Retrieved 8/2/2014 from http://www.cp-africa.com/2013/09/08/facebook-nigeria/

Elebeke, E(18 January, 2012) Nigeria climbs up in Facebook ranking, Vanguard Newspaper, Retrieved 8/2/2014 from http://www.vanguardngr.com/2012/01/nigeria-climbs-up-in-facebook-ranking/

Grahl, T (2014) The 6 types of social media, Out:think, Retreived, 16/02/2014 from www.ouththinkgroup.com/tips/the6-types-of-social-media

Office of the High Commission on Human Rights (OHCHR) (2011) "Freedom of Expression Everywhere", (2011) Freedom of expression everywhere, including in cyberspace , OHCHR, Retrieved 16/2/2014 from http://www.ohchr.org/EN/NewsEvents/Pages/Freedomofexpressioneverywhere.aspx .

Premium Times (2014,1 february2) BREAKING: Jonathan drops corrupt Aviation Minister, Stella Oduah, 3 others. Retrieved 16/2/2014 from http://premiumtimesng.com/news/155031-breaking-jonathan-drops-corrupt-aviation-minister-stella-oduah-3-others.html

Sahara Reporters (2013, October 16) Nigeria's Minister of Aviation Armored BMW

Car Scandal: Car Sells For Only $170K In Europe And America, Sahara Reporters. Retrieved 16/2/2014 from http://saharareporters.com/news-page/nigerias-minister-aviation-armored-bmw-car-scandal-car-sells-only-170k-europe-and-america

TechLoy (2012) Nigeria Crosses 6 Million Facebook Users, Overtakes South Africa [STATS] Retrieved 16/2/2014 from http://techloy.com/2012/10/21/nigeria-crosses-6-million-facebook-users-overtakes-south-africa-stats/

Tiwari, S. and Gosh, G. (2013) Social Media and Freedom of Speech and Expression: Challenges before the Indian law, Retrieved 8/02/2014 from www.academia.edu/4117408/Social_Media_and_Freedom_of_Speech_and_Expression_Challenges_before_the_Indian_law

UNESCO (2013) Freedom Of Expression Toolkit: A Guide Students, UNESCO, Retrieved 16/2/2014 from http://unesdoc.unesco.org/images/0021/002186/218618e.pdf .

Wakawa A. S. Daily Trust (3 July 2013) Press freedom and Nigerian journalists, Daily Trust Newspaper. Retrieved 16/2/2014 from http://weeklytrust.com.ng/index.php/opinion/13209-press-freedom-and-nigerian-journalists

Conceptualising Network Politics following the Arab Spring: An African Perspective

Ashu M. G. Solo and Jonathan Bishop

Abstract: Network politics is examined in the context of the Arab Spring. Network politics refers to politics and networks. These networks include the Internet, private networks, cellular networks, telephone networks, radio networks, television networks, etc. Network politics includes the applications of networks to enable one or more individuals or organizations to engage in political communication. Furthermore, network politics includes government regulation of networks. Finally, network politics includes the accompanying issues that arise when networks are used for political communication or when there is government regulation of networks. The domain of network politics includes, but is not limited to, e-politics (social networking for driving revolutions and organizing protests, online petitions, political blogs and vlogs, whistleblower Web sites, online campaigning, e-participation, virtual town halls, e-voting, Internet freedom, access to information, net neutrality, etc.) and applications of other networks in politics (robocalling, text messaging, TV broadcasting, etc.). The definition of this field should significantly increase the pace of research and development in this important field.

Keywords: network politics, Arab Spring, e-politics

Introduction

Technology has brought about many changes in the realm of politics. This is no truer than in the Middle East and North Africa where the Arab Spring became the latest manifestation of the liberating impact of information and communication technology (Tsuma & Mbarika, 2013).

The Internet is having an extreme impact on social and political systems that is unparalleled in the history of humanity. The revolts in the Middle East and North Africa that started after the beginning of 2011 were largely driven by social networks and are often referred to as the "Arab Spring" (Shavitt & Zilberman, 2012). The Arab Spring involved widespread anti-government protests in many Middle Eastern and North African countries including Tunisia, Egypt, Libya, Yemen, Syria, and Bahrain (Bruns, Wilson, Saunders, Kirchhoff, & Nicolai, 2008). The debate about the Arab Spring is embedded within a complex of wider theoretical debates about how new media might affect political outcomes (Aday et al., 2013).

The Arab Spring has brought down governments in Tunisia, Egypt, Libya, and Yemen and is threatening a fifth government in Syria while a large number of forces will continue to play for the loyalty of the people of the region (Kirk, 2012). These revolutions in North Africa have started in large part due to social networking Web sites like Facebook, Twitter, and YouTube. YouTube is an important tool of the Arab Spring, particularly in Syria where the absence of professional journalists has created a need for citizen video (Youmans & York, 2012). Much of the world was able to see the Arab Spring through photographs and videos made by anonymous local citizens with mobile devices such as cellular phones (Cox, 2011). In Arab countries, there were many activists who played a crucial role in the Arab Spring using social networking as a key tool in expressing their thoughts about the wrongful acts committed by the government (Madu & Moguluwa, 2013; Tufekci & Freelon, 2013).

The Arab Spring wasn't the first technology transformed political struggle. The printing press challenged government ideologies too. In the past, the only political engagement for many people involved voting and following news. As a result of the Internet there is more direct participation in politics (McBeth & Robison, 2012). Therefore, it is necessary to develop new paradigms to understand the changing world. Therefore, in this research paper, the authors describe network politics within the Arab Spring. This field was first originated and defined by the authors of this research (Solo & Bishop, 2011).

Network Politics

The authors have coined the term network politics, which refers to politics and networks (Solo & Bishop, 2011). These networks include the Internet, private networks, cellular networks, telephone networks, radio networks, television networks, etc. Network politics includes applications of networks to enable one or more individuals or organizations to engage in political communication including expression, organization, or voting. Furthermore, network politics includes government regulation of networks. Finally, network politics includes the accompanying issues that arise when networks are used for political communication or when there is government regulation of networks. The term e-politics refers to politics and the Internet (Romm-Livermore, 2011). Therefore, e-politics is a subset of network politics. The term e-government refers to the use of information and communication technologies in government operations, access to government data, interactions between government agencies, interactions between government and citizens, and interactions between government and external organizations (Reddick, 2010). Only those e-government applications in the realm of politics, such as e-voting, are in the domain of network politics. The domain of network politics includes, but is not limited to, e-politics (social networking for driving revolutions, social networking for organizing protests, online petitions, online political videos, political blogs, political vlogs, whistleblower Web sites, online campaigning, e-participation, virtual town halls, e-voting, Internet freedom, access to information, net neutrality, etc.) and the applications of other networks in politics (robocalling, text messaging, TV broadcasting, etc.). The scope of research and development in the field of network politics includes applications of networks to enable one or more individuals or organizations to engage in political communication, government regulation of networks, as well as the accompanying issues that occur as a result of the preceding.

A network politics layman activity could be posting a political blog entry, posting online messages about a protest, or posting online videos of government crackdowns on protesters, all of which can use existing software tools. A network politics research and development activity could be studying the characteristics of political bloggers, developing new software tools for organizing political activists, or developing a tool to alert protesters of protest locations.

Impacts of Network Politics in the Arab Spring

One of the most exciting recent developments in network politics occurred in the recent Libyan Revolution against the dictatorship of Col. Moammar Gaddafi. To prevent rebel fighters from communicating, Gaddafi cut off their telephone and Internet service. Mr. Ousama Abushagur and his team of engineers hived off part of the Libyan cellular phone network and rewired it to run independently of the regime's control, so rebel fighters are able to communicate with cellular phones again (Piaggesi, Sund, & Castelnovo, 2010).

Most collective actions in the Arab Spring had comparable forms of online action, such as online petitions and online fundraising (Rao, 2012). International mobilization through online petitions has denounced human rights violations (Della Porta & Mosca, 2005). The need for more socially responsible investment is also being discussed as essential to addressing the human and environmental needs in the post-Arab Spring Middle East and North Africa (Maestri, 2012). The Arab Spring and calls for democracy in the Middle East and North Africa provide new evidence that the idea of democracy has a global appeal (Anker, 2013). As a huge number of political uprisings and internal conflicts have erupted in the Middle East and North Africa, the Arab Spring shows the importance of the rule of law in ensuring the stability of the international community (Anker, 2013). During the revolution in Egypt in spring 2011, the state television headquarters in Egypt was the first site secured by the Supreme Council of Armed Forces (SCAF) (Saleh, Brevini, Hintz, & McCurdy, 2013). Using social media tools, a political debate television series was created by BBC Arabic and citizen producers in spring 2010. During the Arab Spring, Twitter has been used as a source of information and to coordinate protests and bring awareness to the atrocities (Kumar, Liu, Mehta, & Subramaniam, 2014; Mehta & Subramaniam, 2013). Twitter users commenting on the Arab Spring formed a public sphere. By using common hash-tags such as "#egypt" or "#libya" in their tweets, Twitter users linked their comments to the wider debate (Bruns, Highfield, & Burgess, 2013).

Conclusion

The definition of the new field of network politics will increase the pace of research and development in this extremely important field. Recent events have demonstrated how important this field is. These recent events include recent revolutions in the Middle East and North Africa that were in large part organized using social networking tools such as Facebook and Twitter.

References

Aday, S., Farrell, H., Freelon, D., Lynch, M., Sides, J., & Dewar, M. (2013). Watching from afar media consumption patterns around the Arab Spring. American Behavioral Scientist, 57(7), 899-919.

Anker, T. B. (2013). Power to the people: An essay on branding and global democracy. In R. Varey, & M. Pirson (Eds.), Humanistic marketing (pp. 204). New York, NY: Palgrave Macmillan.

Bruns, A., Wilson, J. A., Saunders, B. J., Kirchhoff, L., & Nicolai, T. (2008). Australia's political blogosphere in the aftermath of 2007 federal election. Paper presented at the Internet Research 9.0: Rethinking Community, Rethinking Place, Copehagen, DK.

Bruns, A., Highfield, T., & Burgess, J. (2013). The Arab spring and social media audiences English and Arabic twitter users and their networks. American Behavioral Scientist, 57(7), 871-898.

Cox, L. P. (2011). Truth in crowdsourcing. Security & Privacy, IEEE, 9(5), 74-76.

Della Porta, D., & Mosca, L. (2005). Global-net for global movements? A network of networks for a movement of movements. Journal of Public Policy, 25(1), 165-190.

Kirk, J. A. (2012). Back to the sea: US strategic requirements and sea control No. ADA561273). Philadelphia, PA: The U.S. Army War College.

Kumar, S., Liu, H., Mehta, S., & Subramaniam, L. V. (2014). From tweets to events: Exploring a scalable solution for twitter streams (No. arXiv:1405.1392). Ithaca, NY: Cornell University.

Madu, R., & Moguluwa, S. C. (2013). Will the social media lenses be the framework for sustainable development in rural Nigeria? Journal of African Media Studies, 5(2), 237-254.

Maestri, E. (2012). The gulf in the southern Mediterranean. In E. Maestri (Ed.), Ideational and material power: The role of turkey and the gulf cooperation council (pp. 1-9). Rome, IT: Istituto Affari Internazionali.

McBeth, M. K., & Robison, S. K. (2012). Introduction to American government: What is it good for? absolutely everything. Journal of Political Science Education, 8(3), 271-287.

Mehta, S., & Subramaniam, L. V. (2013). Tutorial: Social media analytics. Lecture Notes in Computer Science, 8302(2013), 1-21.

Piaggesi, D., Sund, K., & Castelnovo, W. (Eds.). (2010). Global strategy and practice of E-governance: Examples from around the world. Hershey, PA: IGI Global.

Rao, A. (2012). "Sister-groups" and online-offline linkages in networked collective action: A case study of the right to information movement in India. The Electronic Journal of Information Systems in Developing Countries, 52(7), 1-17.

Reddick, C. G. (Ed.). (2010). Politics, democracy, and E-government: Participation and service delivery. Hershey, PA: Information Science Reference.

Romm-Livermore, C. (Ed.). (2011). E-politics and organizational implications of the internet: Power, influence and social change. Hershey, PA: IGI Global.

Saleh, I., Brevini, B., Hintz, A., & McCurdy, P. (2013). Wikileaks and the Arab spring: The twists and turns of media, culture and power. In B. Brevini, A. Hintz & P. McCurdy (Eds.), Beyond WikiLeaks: Implications for the future of communications, journalism and society (pp. 245-253). Basingstoke, GB: Palgrave Macmillan.

Shavitt, Y., & Zilberman, N. (2012). Arabian nights: Measuring the Arab internet during the 2011 events. Network, IEEE, 26(6), 75-80.

Solo, A. M. G., & Bishop, J. (2011). The new field of network politics. Paper presented at the 2011 International Conference on E-Learning, E-Business, Enterprise Information Systems & E-Government (EEE'11), Las Vegas, NV. pp. 442-444.

Tsuma, C. K., & Mbarika, V. W. A. (2013). Understanding the effects of information communication technology and politics: A synthesized analysis of political participation in Kenya. In C. U. Nwokeafor, & K. Langmia (Eds.), Media role in African changing electoral process: A political communication perspective (pp. 171-197). Lanham, MD: University Press of America.

Tufekci, Z., & Freelon, D. (2013). Introduction to the special issue on new media and social unrest. American Behavioral Scientist, 57(7), 843-847.

Youmans, W. L., & York, J. C. (2012). Social media and the activist toolkit: User agreements, corporate interests, and the information infrastructure of modern social movements. Journal of Communication, 62(2), 315-329.

Index

www.ingramcontent.com/pod-product-compliance
Lightning Source LLC
Chambersburg PA
CBHW080237270326

41926CB00020B/4276